A HARVEST
OF
REFLECTIONS

A HARVEST

OF

REFLECTIONS

WISDOM FOR THE SOUL
THROUGH THE SEASONS

Justin Matott

ILLUSTRATED BY
DEBORAH CHABRIAN

BALLANTINE BOOKS
New York

A Ballantine Book
Published by The Ballantine Publishing Group

Copyright © 1998 by Justin Matott
Illustrations © 1998 by Deborah Chabrian

http://www.randomhouse.com

Grateful acknowledgment is made to A.P. Watt Ltd. for permission to reprint an
excerpt from "The Song of Wandering Aengus" from *The Collected Poems of W.B. Yeats*.
Reprinted by permission of A.P. Watt Ltd., on behalf of Michael Yeats.

Library of Congress Cataloging-in-Publication Data
Matott, Justin.
A harvest of reflections : wisdom for the soul through the seasons /
Justin Matott.—1st ed.
p. cm.
ISBN 0-345-42091-8 (alk. paper)
I. Gardens—Religious aspects—Meditations.   2. Gardening—Religious
aspects—Meditations.   3. Matott, Justin.   I. Title.
BL624.2.M36   1999
635—DC21   97-46879
CIP

Manufactured in the United States of America

First Edition: October 1998

10 9 8 7 6 5 4 3 2 1

FOR

Dad

CONTENTS

CONTENTS

ACKNOWLEDGMENTS

IT TAKES A LIFETIME to write a book. There are so many people in my life who have blessed me with friendship, wisdom, a love for life, and an understanding that under this human skin we are all basically the same; I remember and thank you all.

To all whom I've met in passing in bookstores, airplanes, airports, train stations, coffeehouses, nurseries, gardens, and automobiles, thank you for sharing your stories and a small piece of your lives with me.

To those of you kind enough to send letters regarding your impressions of *My Garden Visits*, I thank you; the letters sit in cigar boxes on my desk, there to remind me.

Thank you to all the wonderful booksellers—particularly those who first supported me—and to all the readers, neighbors, and friends who participated in this celebration of life.

To Andy, for all things that you add to my life, which are considerable, immeasurable!

To J.J. and Ethan and the "glue" between us that holds our lives together.

To Julia Nickel Matott, for her eternal gift of love to me and my family.

To the memories of Quentin Scobel and Ann Engle.

To Lionel Matott for a lovely outlook on the world.

To Maribeth (NayNay) and Ron (Coda, write about Cuba) Harris for loving me as a son and especially for having Andy.

To Aunt Renee Lampshire for "reading" my work to

Grandma Elizabeth Harris—an ever-faithful source of enthusiasm and excitement for whatever is next.

To "the Denver legal fan club": Lyla Thiemet, Evelyn Fox, and Mary Hamilton.

To Claudia Henderson and the Zumdieck video fan club in Seattle.

To Erik Judson and John Woods Jr. for constant encouragement, and to Kristin Larsen for friendship, manure, and keeping my "numbers" there while I wrote.

To Scott Ward for sushi, cigars, manure, conversation, and embodying what a "best friend" is.

To Jacques de Spoelberch, my gracious agent, for all you do.

To Judith Curr and to Elizabeth Zack for making me work toward a better book, and to Liz Williams, Rachel Tarlow Gul, Jim Geraghty, Min Choi, Regina Su, and all the wonderful Ballantine people for "getting me out there."

And to Deborah Chabrian for adding a beautiful vision to this book.

Ah yes, and to Snickers of course.

HER GARDEN

This was her dearest walk last year. Her hands
Set all the tiny plants, and tenderly
Pressed firm the unfamiliar soil; and she
It was who watered them at evening time.
She loved them; and I too, because of her.
And now another June has come, while I
Am walking in the shadow, sad, alone.
Yet when I reach the rose-path that was hers,
And breathe the fragrancy of bud and bloom,
She stands beside; the murmur of the leaves,
The well-remembered rustle of her gown,
And low her whisper comes, "My dear! My dear!"
This is her garden. Only she and I—
But always we—may walk its hallowed ways;
And all the thoughts she planted in my heart,
Sunned with her smile, and chastened with her tears,
Again have blossomed—love's perennials.

—Eldredge Denison

WHEN I WAS A CHILD, my father told me once that the roots of the towering old cottonwood tree in our back yard reached clear through to China. I remember wondering if the roots of the trees on the other side of the world somehow poked their way through to our soil too, becoming the branches of a tree over here. Or did the roots meet somewhere in the middle of the earth, holding everything unseen together? To me, roots are the unseen miracles of the wondrous trees and plants around us. A tree, like a human being, allows us to physically view only the showy surface; we rarely see the wonders that lie below.

At the edge of my garden are apple trees, positioned next to a place where I often toil for many hours. Daily I see the transformation that takes place in them. In early spring, the tiny green emerges, forming diminutive leaves and buds, and then blossoms of pink and white clusters; in summer, the blossoms transform into small clusters of fruit; in autumn, golden, green, and red fruits ripen, and the green leaves turn to bronze and red; and finally in winter, the leaves, having fallen, leave the tree barren, void of any apparent signs of life yet awaiting their spring debut once again. The apple trees represent well the cycles of life, and yet all throughout the seasons of change, it is in the roots that life is stored.

Trees speak of something lasting, something constant

and enduring. Planting a tree is somewhat contrary to what our society usually values: instant gratification and immediate results. To plant a tree is to concentrate more on the future than on the present, to gift a legacy for future generations. When I traveled through the mystical redwood forests of northern California, I was given a glimpse into a majestic legacy that began centuries before. The trees there have endured throughout many years, predating the generations of people that currently live there. When I drove down a winding road that cut through the behemoths, I caught a glimpse of just what the majesty of God's garden must be like. Yet the thing that amazed me most about the giants was the fact that their root systems are relatively shallow compared to their enormous show. They hold fast because they colonize, threading their roots together to hold them firmly in the ground. Families joined together by common bonds, determined to hold fast regardless of any storm confronting them. As new members join in with the ancient, their roots intermingle to assure their steadfast place as well.

Everything in the garden is analogous to our lives as a whole. Our life cycles, with all their disappointments, victories, challenges, and simple routines of daily living, are represented well within the boundaries of a garden, often spilling out of the tidy borders. The end of a garden signals seasons to come; first there is autumn, then there is dormancy for a time, but still there is life. There is something very beautiful about the dormancy of the earth, something lovely about the slowing and the contemplation.

INTRODUCTION

The following vignettes are reflections of those things often dormant; like composted material returning to the soil to replenish and rejuvenate for future harvest, these reflections hopefully offer simple truths, lessons, and memories. It should be our firm desire to pass on life's truths and beauty to our children, and to leave a positive imprint on those alongside whom we will journey, and on all those whose paths we have yet to cross. Life is a cycle of continuing patterns and as they say, if we don't learn from history, we are bound to repeat it.

Roots down!

MY GARDEN

A garden is a lovesome thing, God wot!
Rose plot,
Fringed pool,
Ferned grot—
The veriest school
Of peace; and yet the fool
Contends that God is not—
Not God! in gardens when the eve is cool?
Nay, but I have a sign;
'Tis very sure God walks in mine.

— T. E. Brown

THROUGHOUT THIS BOOK you will note poems written by a man named Lionel Matott. My uncle Lionel suffered in his life here with severe cerebral palsy, but he was afflicted in body only. As with others who have maladies affecting the body, my uncle had a brilliant mind. He had a love for mingling words and ink into poetry. He articulated things with a poet's pen that he was unable to act upon physically. Unfortunately, through cruel circumstances, his life was cut short. I have found his beautiful thoughts and poems that remain to be simple, moving, and fitting for this book. My father gave me a small book of Uncle Lionel's poetry called *A Collection of Poems* by Lionel A. Matott. Uncle Lionel dedicated his collection as follows:

The poems in this little volume represent some of the happiest and brightest hours of my life, and the best is none too good to share with my friends. To the ones whose strong arms I have leaned upon, holding them to the slow pace of the crippled while comrades ran by; to the ones whose cheery smiles and willing hands and whose fellowship have been to me as a brother and sister; and to the ones who have patiently borne with my shortcomings while they guided my feet in the paths of learning, I respectfully dedicate this little book as an emblem of my love and gratitude.

Through adversity, beauty springs forth. It is the compost of hardship that enriches the soil after all.

TO THE FALLING LEAVES

Why fall ye, on a day like this?
August is rivaling sweet June's bliss,
The birds are singing their sweetest song,
The honey-bee hums the whole day long,
Breezes ramble o'er the grassy mead,
Meek lowing herds on the hillside feed,
The jolly brook laughs its merry way
Through green fields to the peaceful bay,
All the world bursting into song,
Nature's joys of summer prolong.

Yet silently, as one tired of quest,
One by one, ye fall, and sink to rest;
The only sign in air or on the ground
That autumn soon will hush each sound.

—Lionel A. Matott

A HARVEST
OF
REFLECTIONS

Cucurbita pepo

BOTANICAL NAME

Pumpkin

COMMON NAME

Pumpkin seeds can be sown directly into fertile soil in hills or in wide rows. They enjoy the warm sunny months. The plants spread expansively and are best suited to a garden if planted at least four feet apart. They produce long vines and slow-growing fruits. Pumpkins ripen in the early autumn months to a beautiful orange; harvest them when the skin shows ripe color and hardness of texture. To ensure longer storage capability, leave several inches of dry stem on the fruit. The fruit can be harvested for jack-o'-lanterns, and the pulpy meat can be used in pies and other tasty dishes.

When I was a child, my family would spread newspapers out on the kitchen floor and then we would all take turns imaginatively drawing faces on our designated pumpkins before carving into them. The first year that I was allowed to carve my own pumpkin, I took great pride in using my own Swiss Army knife; it had been a special rite-of-passage, a birthday gift from my father. I carved out an angry-faced pumpkin man as perfectly as possible. Now my sons, equipped with their own Swiss Army knives, carve their own pumpkins into faces that reflect their own moods and inspirations.

As I sit working in my den, I notice that the grass outside is showing signs of turning toward winter. The earth is slowing, preparing for harsher months to come. The drying branches of the pumpkin patch at the back of the vegetable garden signal that, finally, summer is over. A deep pang of regret, mixed with relief in some ways, crosses my mind. The pumpkins, gourds, and tomatoes painting bright oranges, yellows, and reds across the garden are changing the landscape and preparing for the oncoming autumn. The leaves on the bushes and trees are tinged lightly with blanched shades of green not there a mere week ago. They will ease to yellow, and then other colors will follow, until they depart the branches and float to the earth.

Rain now laps at the windows and runs down them in great streaks. The gutters vibrate, with gallons of water rushing down them and spilling into foamy lips at the edge of the lawn. Lightning crosses the sky angrily; its sharp yellow streaks bring memories of summer. The billowing clouds overhead look as though they are great darkening pillows of water, appearing similar to the clouds that will soon bring snow.

The end of August is here. The gardens and the outdoor greenery will become a memory. Soon pumpkins will be carved into gleeful and outrageous faces as the holidays will be upon us again. Harvest time, Halloween, Thanksgiving, Christmas, Hanukkah, New Year's Day. Then there will be Easter, with its lilies and bulbs bursting forth with promises of more gentle days to come. The cycle will continue into the next spring and summer, when once again we will prepare ourselves for another season of life.

Autumn is a time of change, possibly second only to spring as the most animated change the earth undertakes in its cycle of seasons. I have been told that in ancient times it was believed that the time of harvest was when the veil between the two worlds, corporeal and ethereal, was the most thin, allowing for all kinds of mystical occurrences on earth. I don't know if this is true or not for all, but the autumn has always seemed to herald a transformation in my life, as it does for the earth itself.

To a gardener, the coming of the autumnal equinox marks a shift in activity and focus. The summer, spent tending to vegetables, herbs, flowers, and trees—and always, weeds—becomes an almost constant avocation. The seasonal transition brings variety, and often a relief when the gardens stop producing. With the onset of dormancy, the gardener is forced to other activities.

When I was a child in my parents' home, autumn always was a time of great activity. My father and I would spend countless hours harvesting the garden and presenting my mother's kitchen with the plentiful bounty of our collective effort.

I remember well one year as a young boy. After a full

summer of gardening with my father, I set out to harvest a long, mounded row of potatoes under a crisp autumn sky. My father gave me a quick lesson on how to use a digging fork without damaging the crop. I watched the ease with which he turned the soil, then attempted to replicate his enviable one-foot technique. I hadn't yet the weight to use the digging fork in the same manner, so I set it in the ground and jumped onto it with both feet. I ended up sprawled on the ground. My father wryly chuckled and after giving me a few more instructions, he sent me out to harvest from the long row. Within a few minutes I began to scream—a blood-curdling, wake-the-neighbors, send-the-dog-scurrying scream. My father's face was panicked as he bolted from the house and rushed to the garden, sure that I had run one of the spikes from the digging fork through my foot. As he hurried to my side his face melted from a harsh and concerned countenance to one of relief and amazement. In my hands I held a potato larger and more misshapen than any he or I had ever seen; it was roughly the same size as my head. My father put his arm about my shoulder and squeezed me in tightly, relieved and delighting in my excitement. I think it was then that we both realized that a passion for the soil would be a shared devotion between us, a common ground.

Three decades later, my garden holds the remnants of some of my father's floral efforts. Near the front door of our house are clumps of iris that began in the gardens of my childhood home. As the love for gardening was such an important early connecting point for my father and myself, I hoped that the same would hold true for my sons and me. At this point my sons aren't quite as enthusiastic about the toiling as my father and I were, so to inspire them to enjoy the time spent near the earth, I decided to give them a plot in the garden that was their very own. It would be one in which they could plant whatever they wanted, with only my casual assistance and advice.

We visited our favorite local nursery and painstakingly chose the vegetable seed packets that sounded most interesting to the boys. Later, in the vegetable garden, as I carefully laid out a line of twine between two stakes to show them how to follow uniformly, "correctly," within the row, I heard the sounds of ripping and giggling behind me. I turned to find that my sons had torn the top off all the seed packets and were delighting in mixing the seeds of spinach, carrot, lettuce, peas, radishes, and chard all together into a small pail. Shortly thereafter, seeds that were supposed to be spaced apart by feet—not by eighths of an inch, according to the backs of the seed packets—were tumbling together into a foot-wide path that we had dug out of the soil. Several weeks later, a cornucopia of color appeared among my otherwise spaced lines of vegetables. Though the row that my boys planted didn't yield as many vegetables as it might have that summer, the boys had enjoyed themselves in the garden, and it was their row that my neighbors and friends commented on most. By my letting them create that little oasis of nonconformity and not stifling their desire, my sons came closer to the passion of the soil that I shared as a boy with my own father.

Since that time, I haven't used either twine or stakes myself. I now notice that my own lines are rarely straight and spaced exactly, and I am no longer bothered by it.

I think back to autumns past. Although I myself did not grow up on a farm, I did grow up in the country, and many of my school friends lived on farms. I particularly enjoyed visiting my friends' farms in the season of change. We would speed down dirt lanes on our Sting-Ray bicycles with banana seats and long sissy bars that waved over our heads. The lanes would be filled with leaves of many colors that would crackle and billow as we passed through.

My friends and I would collect enormous piles of the leaves and jump into them. Always meeting our eyes were fields of corn with drying golden husks. At the edges of the fields would be great plantings of pumpkins. We would steal our way into the fields, pulling corn cobs off the stalks, husking them, and chewing the dry corn off the cobs. As the leaves of the pumpkin plants dried and wilted away, the orange fruits of numerous shapes and sizes dotted the land-scape in a checkerboard of color, signaling harvest time.

The pumpkins would be gathered in gigantic piles near the old red-gray barns or displayed handsomely on the backs of the hay wagons. The hay wagons would soon be used for rides through the chilling autumn nights, as neighbors and friends joined together to enjoy the celebration of bounty.

The rain begins to lift and the sun comes out again, warming the newly replenished plants. To the east arises a beautiful double rainbow. I now think it a good time to examine the remaining vegetables in the diminishing garden. I step out of the house to the refreshing smell of rain and the earthy scents created by the mixture of soil and water, as the clouds drift eastward. As I enter the center of the vegetable garden, I note two pitiful pumpkins, mostly forgotten at the back of the vegetable garden. For most of the summer months they were covered by abundant, thick squash plants and cucumber vines that had found their way across the entire back quarter; now the squash and vines are withering and wilting under the weight of the rainwater and autumn's chill, allowing for the full viewing of the little globes.

I realize that I need to go to a nearby pumpkin patch to get fodder for the season's festivities and jack-o'-lanterns. An embarrassing thing to admit to the boys—their father a braggadocio gardener, able to produce nary a pumpkin of any substance. The thought of selecting the largest pumpkins from a nearby farmer's patch and secretly ferreting them into the soil at the back of the garden under the vines occurs to me. But I place the pumpkins, purchased secretly, on the front porch instead, and let my boys draw their own conclusions as to the origin of the giants.

As I think again of the upcoming holiday season, I am reminded of a time when, in junior high school, I was invited to a traditional Halloween party in a barn. The Halloween evening was spent in traditional play—dunking for sweet red apples, throwing horseshoes, playing games of truth or dare, spinning the bottle. It ended in a sweet kiss in the hayloft for me, from a young girl known as Lisa. For years after that kiss I remembered the smell of the hay and the aromas of the barn mixing together. She had smelled of the barn, her hair of hay, leather, horses, sweat, and sweet oats. Her breath had been fresh, like freesia. Things earthy and innocent had met as our noses collided in a clumsy kiss.

Whimsical, how the kiss meant so much at the time. A rite-of-passage. Her father had had nothing to worry about from me, a fumbling teenager with absolutely no intention or wherewithal of going beyond a kiss with his pretty young daughter. The kiss and subsequent innocent kisses over the next few months had sustained me, tantalizing my fantasies about the opposite sex for a time. I had lain awake in my room imagining the possibility of our future spent together— a plan she had never shared. The imaginings of this young man ended abruptly when she found my older brother more compatible for a time.

Still, in that autumn of my first romance, Lisa gave me a large uncarved pumpkin as a party favor. It was lopsided and weighed about ten pounds. I kept it in my room, a token of our relationship, until it began to smell like fetid pumpkin pie and my mother insisted on its joining the compost pile in the back yard. Lisa was not to stay in my life for long, but during an autumn many years later, filled with hay rides, Halloween dances, and romance, my heart was captured by a most remarkable young woman. She and I have been carving pumpkins together every year since.

AUTUMN

Autumn is a glorious time,
I love it, yes I do;
I love to wake and find the grass,
All white with frosty dew.

O! for the days of autumn,
With sunshine bright and clear;
And on the trees of woodlands,
Bright new dresses appear.

Let me wander in forests,
With nuts upon the ground
And you can have the wonders,
Of any modern town.

I love the golden hours,
When nature smiles its last;
And in the woods and meadows,
Blushing youth is past.

—Lionel A. Matott

Malus
BOTANICAL NAME

Dwarf Apple Tree
COMMON NAME

The apple tree flourishes where a chilly winter will prepare it for fruit bearing. It adds beauty and contrast to gardens, along with delicious fruit in the autumn. An apple tree prefers fertile loam in full sun, although some varieties can be domesticated in tubs. The apple tree can be grown in a dwarf variety in most yards. With a dwarf tree, the harvesting of the fruit is made easier, and often the trees bear within a season of planting. Nothing in the stores can replicate an apple picked fresh from your own tree.

The apple tree has been maligned because of the common thought of its being what the serpent used to deceive the first humans in the original garden. In reality, in that kind of climate, the serpent probably would have given Eve a mango.

The Golden Delicious apples at the corner of my garden are now readying for harvest. A kiss from the retreating sun illuminates the top side of each apple, leaving a slight pink tinge on each upturned "face." This new color is the last change the apples will experience before they depart from the tree that has sustained their life over a year of seasons. From a tiny seed has come forth an abundance of fruit that will produce a kitchen of activity: caramel apples, apple pie, applesauce, apple juice—so many things from one little seed.

I SPENT ONE OF THE LAST SUNRISES of the summer in my garden; the earth was rapidly heeding the warnings of oncoming cold. The garden was showing a final attempt; rare and beautiful colors were cast across the plantings, green bell peppers slowly turning red, turning their composition to a much sweeter flavor.

Drawn in by the garden's peacefulness, my mind drifted to the thought of the garden as the most universal metaphor for life God has created. That He started it all in a garden is not by coincidence, as any lover of a garden will tell you! In the garden, life, in all its cycles, is represented.

The apple tree before me had come forth from the desolate dormancy of last winter to a celebration of diminutive pink buds this past spring. Soon those buds had been replaced by fragrant flowers and leaves that adorned the tree through the summer season. Apples were now growing slowly in the cool snap of autumn evenings, until delectable fruit came forth.

In many ways the apple tree is a symbol of autumn's bounty and harvest, yet it is more truly representative of the culmination of a series of seasons, ending with a final blaze of show before dormancy is brought upon the tree by the changing of the season once again. The apple tree shows its greatest splendor and beauty in its last season, before the "death" of winter quiets it.

Often we ourselves experience a last change before death that is like the change and spectacular show that trees in autumn undergo. In the last months and years we spend on earth as mortals we can realize the fruition of plans long desired. Like the trees, individuals will often allow the eccentricity that has been within them since childhood to show forth on their "branches" once again. People will become what they were intended to be without regard for others' opinions; they will engage in, if you will, a second childhood.

As a teenager, I volunteered in a retirement community, where I watched the elderly returning to play the same way they had as children and reveling in the glory days of their youth. Uninhibited laughter and frivolity were the tone of many there. Although I had to endure the sad deaths of some of those friends, I was able to see that the wisdom of age and gray hair seemed for many as consent to live again in a second, well-deserved, childhood. I remember two people most particularly. One was a tiny woman named Nelly who possessed a thick New England accent and who was convinced somehow that I was her husband, Jonas, a man she hadn't heard from since he had apparently gone out to sea some decades earlier, never to return. I went along with it and called myself Jonas as we walked arm in arm down the corridors of the retirement community. I found it embarrassing and silly at first, and then somehow it became as easy for me as it was necessary for her.

Then there was Jake, a huge man confined to a wheelchair who still believed that he was running a large ranch somewhere up in the frigid northern states and that I was one of the overseers of his oil and cattle operations. He would call out to me from his room as I slunk by, usually admonishing me for forgetting to do something, like chipping the ice off the cattle's water tubs or mending some barbed-wire fence. Always he was there with several more chores for me to do.

Jake and Nelly had both returned to the happiest times of their lives; they were somehow free from the worries of life that most of us were caught up in and had selected the best of their pasts in which to revel. Considering the changes that had come to them in their lives, I recognized that their perspectives were a gift that they had received to make their last years more content and happy.

When I was a much younger boy, I spent time with a woman who lived down the dirt lane behind our home. She was a kind, wrinkled old woman with a large bun of salt-and-pepper gray hair, a stooped back, sacklike dresses, a straw hat, and an infectious enthusiasm for the earth. She was in her "twilight years" and had through many decades learned what is important in life. One of those things was children: she welcomed my friends and me into her back yard to dig for fishing worms; she paid us for little chores; and she invited us to simply sit a spell over lemonade and ginger cookies. She was like Mr. McGregor of "Peter Rabbit" fame—only with charity and love for the small ones underfoot. With wisdom and a genteel nature harvested over time, she had learned along the way what was to be the focus of her life.

Widowed for many years at the point that I made her acquaintance, she had let her large back gardens go fallow, with one great exception: her berries. She had the largest strawberry bed I have ever seen, and at the end of her property she had numerous rows of abundant gooseberry thickets and raspberries. She always let us pick berries and eat them until we were stuffed. Mrs. Engle made a lasting impression on my life, and I remember thinking, never having known my own grandparents, that spending time with her must be what it would be like to have had them with me.

A cool breeze floated through the yard, bringing me back to the present. I shivered and pulled my sweatshirt tighter about my neck. Looking at the heavy apples on the trees, I realized that soon the branches would become barren again.

As I collected several baskets of apples, yellow and red, I became fully aware of the transition that had taken place in them through their seasons of life. The fulfillment of their purpose and the many uses of the "talents" they possessed within were soon to be enjoyed by others. Each individual, yet quite similar to one another. No two exactly alike. William Butler Yeats wrote, "And pluck till time and times are done/The silver apples of the moon,/The golden apples of the sun." And I plucked until they were safely in my storage, each with a purpose fulfilled.

It is said that when Johnny Appleseed was a man advanced in age he was still set on delivering the legacy of his dream of bringing apples to all those he encountered along the way. In a time when survival was paramount and the frontier was rugged, his simple dream was to have apple trees cast about the landscape. How many eyebrows he must have raised with his eccentric outlook on what in life in the rugged frontier was important ... but what a wonderful legacy he left through the fruits of his experience.

Crataegus phaenopyrum

BOTANICAL NAME

Washington Hawthorn

COMMON NAME

The Washington hawthorn is native to the United States and can be transplanted from containers or balled and burlaped. The trees prefer full sun in fertile, loamy soil. They possess sharp thorns on their branches and will reach heights of forty feet. Through pruning, they can be molded into a beautiful flowering hedge. In the spring they are covered with white blossoms; in the autumn they yield brilliant carmine-red berries.

Off the elevated back of the deck from our home my wife and I set a hawthorn tree years ago within an arm's length, so that one day it would grow as a canopy of sorts, providing us with shade, color, and privacy. In the autumn we would observe and enjoy the small birds that came to peck at the carmine berries, and in the spring we would enjoy the blossoms, like clusters of living bouquets at eye level. As I sat one day on the back porch, two small birds kept flitting in and out of the lower branches of the tree. Soon it was apparent that it was to be the new home for their young. My wife and I watched in wonder as the eggs cracked and the young birds grew under the watchful and cautious eye of their mother. Too soon it was time for them to leave the nest to start their own families. All things in life have an order, and the easing of the seasons represents this well.

LEAVES CASCADE ACROSS THE YARD with every breath of breeze now. The berries on the hawthorn that is huddled close to the house are more apparent today than yesterday as each leaf takes leave of its place. I look at the tree with an entirely different perspective when below it, in the garden, than from my usual view, up on the deck. I see the tree from the trunk up, rather than only the mid- and top-level branches that peek above the patio deck. I am reminded of the story of the blind men giving a description of an elephant; inspecting it from very different places, each had his own conception and version of the great beast. So with the hawthorn tree; the complexities and unique swirling of the bark and the sedum and the pansies that surround the base of the tree are not evident from my other view above.

Trees all about me hung with autumn fruit, walnuts, and berries. Autumn harvest was in full gear. A familiar cool snap permeated the air, indicating the seasonal changes taking place. Apples, pumpkins, gourds, grapes, cucumbers, and other cool-weather vegetables needed to be gathered and stored for use over the long, dormant winter. I pulled the last of the cucumbers from their drying branches and filled several large colanders and a basket with the green tomatoes that had little hope of ripening on the vine with the snap of cold in the air. The redolent smell of several decomposing apples beneath the trees wafted in the slightly warming air like sweetly scented potpourri. The squirrels had knocked the apples off the tree over the late summer months and the partially eaten cores lay near the base of the trees, slowly returning to the soil.

The weather forecasters had warned of temperatures in the low thirties for the following days, and the aspen trees' leaves had been turning for weeks in the lower foothills and now in my yard as well. It was time to take most of the garden apart and prepare myself again for a long season void of the soil on my hands and the contemplation of the space for quiet. (And in fact, the temperature did drop considerably for several days. But had I the foresight to simply cover the garden with blankets, I would have been the wiser! The sun returned in a hot ball in the sky and we enjoyed four weeks of weather reaching the low eighties.) The garden would have had another month of life in which to bring forth its bounty, but like so many people who do not perceive the healing and warmth that tomorrow might bring, I ended it too soon. I only wonder what could have become of the plantings had they been left to their intended days. Current circumstances can cloud the eyes of so many to the promise of future sunrises and life's inevitable changes. If only the foresight for tomorrow's possibilities had been weighed.

A familiar presence felt near. I sensed a metaphorical association between her presence and that of the harvest: both had left rich legacies. My life had changed forever as a result of the garden's gifts and the lessons I derived from my mother's visits to my garden. I spoke aloud, thanking my mother for her rich legacy, but suddenly I felt very alone. A chill, as though it were physical, swept through the yard, and it was the clearest moment since she left this earth physically that I felt the enormous void in my life from her departure. I longed for her presence with the same strength that I had on the night that she passed away.

The earth that I had turned inward, rich and black, smelled of the essence of life. As I crouched down between tall tomato plants, green and reddening peppers, and purple-black eggplants, ready for harvest, completely "lost" in my garden, I again felt a sensation overcome me. She *was* there with me once again. The feeling her presence brought to my heart—the comfort it gave—was like awakening on a spring morning with the meadowlark's and robin's songs. As her presence increased, I thought back on the first visit that I had with her in my garden. So many things had changed as a result of those meetings and their insights. My family and I are closer as a family now, and the assurances of the hereafter she brought make living in the present more meaningful than before. The anticipation of her next potential insights brings a value to my every day and every interaction.

I heard a "whisper," and my heart jumped. I felt her comforting presence as I had several years before and which I had described in my previous book, *My Garden Visits*. I had thought of her so much lately as a result of losing another close friend, his loss a reminder of how little guarantee we have of time here and how important it is to spend each day as though it were our last.

Quentin had lived with the knowledge for ten years that he would lose his battle for life. Though only in his thirties, he, like so many people of advanced age and wisdom, set out to experience and fulfill his dreams. He left behind the normal conventional hold that many feel and allowed his own eccentricity, his individual imprint, to show forth. He built metal sculptures that he placed in the cities in which his sisters lived, a testimony to his having been there. He actively raised funds for his friends in need and exposed those of us with little understanding other than what we see on the news to issues that are affecting most of us now. In short, he lived the last days of his life with as much relish as he could and convinced those around him to do so as well. Though his "autumn" and eventually his "winter" came prematurely, his imprint on those who knew him was perennial.

My mother's communication illuminated to me life's delicate balance and the necessity to draw close to the "soil," to focus on what is vital and important. That life is a successive pattern of seasons and changes and in order to truly relish its magic one must keep in mind that there is a time and a place for all things. That I myself had become possibly too reflective and nostalgic, searching for too much meaning in the past and not giving enough credence to the present and all that it held. Although blessed with an abundant and lovely childhood, the present was where I needed to live and apply to it the lessons of the past. To pass on the lessons to the children in my care as she had with me.

"All things in order, all things in order. . . ." The words came to me through her. Her presence diminished once again, and I was left there with my thoughts. I started to hum a song that I hadn't thought of for many years, a song stating that all things had a season, all things would turn. I left the garden and went into my den, pulling out my Bible and turning to the Old Testament. There it was from many years past—the wisdom of the ages and a clear indication of the balance of nature and humankind in God's economy:

A time to be born; a time to die; A time to plant; a time to harvest; A time to kill; a time to heal; A time to destroy; a time to build; A time to cry; a time to laugh; A time to grieve; a time to dance; A time for scattering stones; a time for gathering stones; A time to hug; a time not to hug; A time to find; a time to lose; A time for keeping; a time for throwing away; A time to tear; a time to repair; A time to be quiet; a time to speak up; A time for loving; a time for hating; A time for war; a time for peace. (Ecclesiasties 3:2–8)

Solomon, an ancient Hebrew king and a proficient writer, made some observances regarding life that have held true through the ages. They teach us to keep everything in balance and perspective. He wrote of his lover in metaphor; the garden was the representation of the deep love that he felt for her in the Song of Solomon. If all the areas of our lives were handled carefully, to focus on balance instead of the polarity that divides us, if we could try to see both sides of issues, we could find the balance that could bring this world peace. Solomon in his wisdom tried to let us know that through the ages "this too shall pass." That the things we often value or dwell upon have little eternal or even temporal meaning. Again I thought on the fact that it is often advanced age that allows the perspective to look back on events and give them their true relevance.

My mother had come to me again in the garden, to remind me of all the great gifts of life that I possessed. Indeed I am a fortunate man, with a loving wife, healthy children, and the benefit of friends and family with whom to share life. *"All things in order, all things in order."* It made sense, the pattern of life. To live in today, to hope for tomorrow, and to remember the past for each day that brought new insight and wisdom and love. As I watch the new buds on the hawthorn tree, I will not wish for the berries; as the berries form, I will not long for the sweet scent of the flowers; and as winter comes to claim the outward growth, I will remember the roots, remember the strength the tree is deriving by returning to its roots.

My sons rounded the house, finding me there in the garden once again, tending and lost in thought. They carried baseball mitts and a ball. It was time to play. *"All things in order, all things in order."*

Acer rubrum

BOTANICAL NAME

Scarlet Maple

COMMON NAME

The scarlet maple is a very adaptable variety of maple. It will do well in most of the northern continent. Even so, the wisdom that applies to the planting of any tree is to select plants that have been grown locally or tempered, hardened so that the tolerance levels have been established for seasonal heat and cold variations. Maples can be added to a yard either as balled and burlaped or bare-root trees. They thrive in moist soil with sun or partial shade, and prefer acidic soil. Medium to fast growing, maple trees add a delightful variety of color to any yard. A definite autumn favorite, the scarlet maple has verdant summer leaves that yield to autumnal oranges and reds in a vibrant show.

A single maple tree stood at the front of my family's first house, furnishing shade and beauty. Its burnt reds in the autumn could be seen from a mile away. Not as indigenous as in eastern cities, the scarlet maple is often a solitary treat in the West, singular among aspen, pines, cottonwood varieties, and others. My parents, both originally from New York State, commented that autumn was the one season that made them homesick for the East; the turning of the aspen trees in the Rocky Mountains is beautiful indeed, but could not compare to the reds, oranges, browns, greens, pinks, and other vibrant colors that densely painted the eastern landscapes each fall.

LIKE A MAPLE TREE standing with its russet leaves framed against an otherwise verdant backdrop, my mother was by all accounts unusual and unique. She, too, was a burnished bush among a forest of green boughs. My mother found her own way in a difficult world and determined that there was nothing in this great nation, in God's great world, that she couldn't accomplish if her desire were great enough.

Now, those of us who knew her well felt different about some of her endeavors ... one of which was singing. Over and over she claimed that she had "perfect pitch." She would sit at the old black upright Steinway in the living room and play as though she were leading a concert. Unfortunately, her singing didn't jibe with the melody coming from the piano; even the dog would leave the room in alarm. Still she would sit down to sing an off-key but heartfelt rendition of some musical piece, undaunted by our criticism. She even joined a chorale where her "perfect pitch" could unite with a hundred other voices and blend in—or be drowned out, as the case may be. I always looked on the people in her row with compassion and slight embarrassment, but they all loved her. Her spirit was one that few possessed, and her passion for the music alone earned her the right to sing with the chorale, whether in tune or not.

That was how my mother was in everything she undertook. She rarely let other people's decisions or prognosis of her situation change her resolve. Even to the end, on the night that we lost her, she showed a determination to hold on for one last message. It was her mind and soul's attempt to overcome a noncooperative body.

She had lain there motionless. A tumult of thoughts invaded my mind, as life drained from her face like water retreating with the tide from the beach. In the same way that the tide goes, she was losing her steady place. For several days we had been sitting watching her body rebel and grimace against itself as the machines puttered, whirred, and kept life flowing through her. As the prognosis for recovery worsened, we were confronted with the reality that her wishes must be honored—that her life not be artificially prolonged when her body shut down, for her spirit no longer desired to stay. Though it was with clear understanding of what we did, I immediately felt orphaned when she drew her last breath and I lost my mother and close friend.

Nearly fifteen years earlier, her body had begun to show signs of breaking down, of going against her wishes. The rapidly increasing frequency of headaches, memory lapses, and outbreaks of violent rage were not normal for her. One day our car drove headlong into the back of another car at around forty miles per hour. I looked at my mother from the back seat and realized that she was asleep in the driver's seat. Shame washed over me as I realized the other kids in the car were also wondering how someone with the responsibility of hauling five kids in a carpool from school could do this.

After months of my mother's experiencing this rapid downslide in her physical and mental health, the doctors finally ordered a brain scan. They found a tumor that had been growing for many years and now was growing exponentially, threatening to kill her within days. I was thirteen years old and, struggling with the onset of puberty, the waking of hormones, suddenly I had a dying mother. And with that knowledge came the realization that the focus of the family and friends would no longer be on me and my brother in our time of need.

I traveled with my father and brother to a large city that had hospitals that would be able to care for my mother in ways that our small town hospital could not. My brother lay in the same strange room with me, away from home, as our mother underwent a frightening evening under the knife of a skillful neurosurgeon. I lay silently, confused and afraid, listening to my brother cry himself to sleep. That night I lost the brother that I had known during my childhood. He changed; it was as if he had purposefully built a wall around himself that nothing would penetrate ever again. But we all changed that night. The next day we saw her in intensive care, her head wrapped in a blood-soaked turban, her face wilted and pulled in ways that I had never seen before. It scared the hell out of me. My mother talked of having traveled through a tunnel of light. Of having seen the other side of our dimension, and that her mission in life was not yet complete. In the midst of otherwise devastating circumstances she had experienced a spiritual renewal, a rejuvenation that she passed on to me.

It wasn't until many years later that the tumor finally made a reappearance. My mother was attending a health club regularly and relishing the gifts of a life that she had nearly lost years before. She was living every day as though it were her last, and educating herself as though she had the promise of another seventy years. She celebrated her evenings with books, good wines, and gourmet foods; when my wife and I would visit, we would always be treated to my mother's favorite dessert: Häagen-Dazs chocolate chip ice cream soaked in Grand Marnier. She would crawl on the ground with her young grandchildren and sing to them the German lullabies from her youth. She would visit Europe frequently because she loved her homeland. And she took the time to pursue things deemed by many as frivolous, or, perhaps, self-indulgent. Yet it was my mother's ability to live out her life uniquely and fully that has left the largest impression on those who knew her. To search out the zest in life, to share deep conversation with a friend, to experience things most only dream about—that is what adds magic to this life. And that is part of what makes our loved one's unique memory live on.

This year I will watch the changing of the maples closely. I will watch the reddish veins creep into the green leaves, changing them casually and forever. As the leaves cling to the mantle from which they first burst and then finally fall to the earth below in a russet carpet, I will harvest some of the leaves—placing a few in between the pages of a favorite book to remind me, when I open it, of the uniqueness of the people I love. For my mother is worthy of volumes of books, but she is just one of the many gems that surround us. We each have the potential to touch others' lives in a special way. How boring the world would be if that were not so.

I was recently told that to become immortal you should write a book, raise a child, or plant a tree. Not everyone has the desire to do the former but everyone can plant a tree. Plant a maple, watch with wonder as it reaches to the heavens, and leave a legacy for future generations.

NOVEMBER NIGHT

Listen ...
with faint dry sounds,
Like steps of passing ghosts,
The leaves, frost-crisp'd, break from the trees
And fall.

—Adelaide Crapsey

(From *The Melody of Earth*)

Cornus sericea

BOTANICAL NAME

Red-twig Dogwood

COMMON NAME

Red-twig dogwood will thrive in various soil compositions and will tolerate even damp soil if given full sun. It can be planted from nursery containers as well as from bare-root planting, or it can be propagated by cuttings. Once the dogwood completes its flowering, it is recommended to prune it to the trunk in the fall to encourage new juvenile stems and to assure good bearing in the following seasons. Planted against light-colored structures, the red-twig dogwood will give off color in all seasons, with oval, serrated leaves and white flowers in spring and summer. In snowy climates selectively prune stems, leaving them to overwinter; this assures beautiful contrasting color to the snow and other winter elements. The deep red will give contrast in borders that are generally spread with green junipers and other constant greenery.

The dogwood at the front of our house provides a beautiful greeting to visitors all year long. In the warmer months, the dogwood is graced with green and variegated leaves that are set off against the red brick of our house; the pretty white flowers of spring grace the tops and give way to the small berries that both decorate the yard and feed the birds that flit about. I can never bring myself to prune a dogwood as much as is suggested. I so enjoy the contrast the branches provide against the snow of winter, a reminder to me of the glorious colors the garden gives during the warmer months.

OFTEN IN THE WARMER MONTHS I go to the back patio to write. Today, despite the crispness of fall, I venture there still. As I have done numerous times before, I bring along my beloved pooch, Snickers, to enjoy the crisp morning air. With her sweet temperament as well as the lining of nuttiness in her personality, Snickers is aptly named.

Every few minutes or so Snickers comes over to me, checking to see if I have decided yet to pull myself away from my work to play with her. She gets annoyed with me; she cannot understand why we sit so close to so many unthrown balls and toys that have somehow accumulated on the porch. Over and over she brings them to me to throw. When I ignore her attempts at play, she sighs loudly and looks at me with her big brown eyes, trying to charm me into interrupting my intentions of work. When I ignore her and simply sit there sipping French Roast coffee, meditating and writing, it unnerves her greatly. She nuzzles my hand until I stop writing and stroke her wiry back. When I stop the petting, she pushes her little wet nose under my arm to coax me to continue.

In a moment I look up and toss a ball to her. Immediately I am forgiven for making her wait, and she is ready to play cheerfully with me. She bounds after the ball readily, often pausing to sniff near the red-twig dogwoods at the side of the house where small cottontail bunnies have found a home.

Not just a play companion, Snickers is also my sometime jogging companion. When she ventures out with me, she follows along merrily, taking in all the scents and sights of the paths we travel on. When we encounter another dog on our jogs, she either greets it with a furiously wagging tail or cowers behind me if the other's greeting seems hostile. This always reminds me of how quickly we withdraw a cheerful greeting when others seem hostile or terse to our display of good cheer!

The way that we greet each other on first meeting has an impact on how we interact throughout our time together. Greetings set the tone for how all the inhabitants of a house will interact. A welcome greeting instead of a fierce complaint about the day makes our interactions easier and more enjoyable.

In my home the one that always beats the rest of my family to the door to greet me is Snickers. When she greets me with her peculiar, upturned-lipped smiles, barks of joy, and overstated tail wagging, I am ensured of my place of importance in her life.

Animals are special additions to families: we humans learn a lot from them about how to love each other. They offer love with no strings attached, for they possess a simple desire to love unconditionally.

A dog's love is something we all could learn from. I can

go into the house for five minutes, and when I return to the porch I receive a greeting from Snickers as though I have been gone all day. What if every day we came in the door and our loved ones greeted us with the same enthusiasm that a dog greets its master? What blessings we would give those in our lives if we greeted them with unconditional love and enthusiasm every time we saw them! To interact with one another with the knowledge that we once again marked another person's life with a positive message would enrich us all and bring peace to this world.

When my children come in from the many adventures of the day, my wife makes them feel special and welcome in our house. It is a place they look forward to returning to from their daily exploits in the neighborhood or from school. As I come to my home every night, I too return to the refuge of my safe place, my home. No matter what I have been through during the day, when I enter the door to my home I am loved and accepted by the people that I hold most dear. I try to remember to greet them with love, respect, and happiness, to assure them well. My sons, for the most part, have learned the value of a welcome greeting and take the time to greet others cheerfully.

Near the entrance of my house the lovely red-twigged dogwoods serve as a greeting to all that come to our home. In the warmer months they provide a cheery greeting of green, white, and red; in the cooler months, they offer a strong contrast of color against a landscape that has become a sterile white and gray. This winter, the twigs of the dogwoods will provide a huge wreath of color on my front door, to remind me as I enter our home to cherish all those who live there.

Populus tremuloides

BOTANICAL NAME

Aspen

COMMON NAME

The aspen, a short-lived and delicate-wooded tree, is a species within the poplar family. A deciduous tree that is found bountifully in the mountains, it can grow to ninety feet in height. Its leaves, green above and silvery below, grow between one to three inches in diameter and have small, rounded teeth. Aspens can be transplanted bare root, or balled and burlaped for larger trees. They prefer full sun and loamy soil to maintain good growth, but will grow in poor soil where most other trees will not. They provide privacy with their fast-growing foliage, allowing the sun to only dapple through their leaves. The characteristic possibly most endearing to the species is the quaking of the leaves with any atmospheric change; the stem of the leaf is suspended in a manner that allows it to rotate in a quaking fashion, appearing as a shimmer in a breeze. When hundreds of aspens are viewed in a soft wind, it is like watching the movements of a symphony.

In the fall the aspen trees brilliantly turn, in contrast to the surrounding pines. When I was a child, I would go on picnics with my family to the mountains. In autumn we particularly enjoyed going to areas densely populated by aspen trees to view the annual change of color. As we walked through the great giants of Colorado, my parents would gather aspen branches, pussy willows, and assorted wild flowers for a display on the Steinway that would then sit with great importance in our living room.

FALL HAD COME to the mountains early this year. Although the leaves there usually turn a month in advance of those in the lowlands where I reside, this particular year had experienced an even earlier onset of cold weather. I felt the need to take one last sojourn into the mountains on my motorcycle unencumbered by the heavy leather chaps and jacket that would be necessary in the oncoming months. I wanted to visit a special place, a place where I had experienced some mystical and enchanting experiences over the past years.

Along the winding road, yellows, oranges, reds, browns, and tans in a symphony of color crisscrossed and dotted the otherwise verdant mountains. Patches of color sprang forth between the tall stands of pine and aspen trees that blanketed many miles of mountains. A slight breeze blew, quaking the aspen trees, threatening to end the splendor of their show if the wind grew too strong. I pulled my motorcycle off the road to take in the overwhelming sights of autumn, my hands complaining of the cooling air even through thick leather gloves.

Fall is a time of change and a time to slow down, to harvest, and to ponder the many lessons learned over the warmer, easier months. The changing of seasons reminds us of the larger seasons of our lives. Reminds us not to wish away the specific magic of each season, but to relish its place as it eases continuously into the next. Each time a season eases aside for the next one to come, there is an opportunity to look forward to new life or to reflect upon the gifts enjoyed in the last season. Most of the plants, both annuals and perennials, retreat, hibernate, or return to the earth that they have been born from to replenish tired soil and allow for newness in a coming season.

I stashed my motorcycle and began my descent into a valley filled with colors. The sun filtered through the golden leaves of the fluttering aspen trees overhead as I walked down a long dirt trail beside a gently flowing creek. A cloak of color surrounded me in the little forest; birds chittered nervously as they readied themselves for a long trip south. The lining of trees reminded me briefly of walks down tree-lined pathways of my youth. A flash of homesickness came and went without allowing me to understand its relevance.

Gravel and dried mud from an earlier rainfall crunched beneath my feet, the only sound among the muted green and vibrant autumn colors except for the occasional call of a blue jay or a magpie and the far-off chatter of small blackbirds. I ventured farther into the back woods, breathed deep the piney nectar, and relished the sun on my face. I hoped the woods around me would inspire words for a novel that I had been laboring over.

The sun's light on the thick forested path allowed just enough heat through to warm me from the chill of autumn in the mountains. The crisp snap in the air burnished the leaves of the aspen trees as they readied themselves for the upcoming brutal cold of the winter. Soon the canvas of greens, oranges, gold, and browns would be replaced by a downy white winter coat. Life would slow, and it would be left to the strong to forage for sustenance.

I recalled a path opening up into the valley, and if memory served me well, a large, possibly abandoned homestead sat in the meadow away from the highway and the confusion of human habitation. The musty smell of damp hay in the valley below reached my nose. The familiar growing smells of farmland penetrated the air as I descended into the meadow, again causing me to wax nostalgic for my youth. The grass waved in great sheets of tawny grain, beckoning me downward.

After a mile or so of venturing along the gravel pathway, I came upon a large barn in the old European style distinct in the valley. The once blood-red sides, now more gray than red, spoke of a simpler life than mine. I imagined the barn when it was raised, the farmer mixing his paints of linseed oil from flax, red oxide, and casein from cow's milk. For a good many years I have wanted to buy a piece of land with an old barn on it and then convert it into a house. This barn has all the markings of my dream barn: it is a Yankee barn, with three bays and a side entrance. Unique to the area, it also has two threshing bays on the opposite side, harkening from early American barns in the East.

I cautiously surveyed the surrounding valley and approached closer to the barn. It became obvious that it was still in use, and it made me long for the day that my "barn dream" will come true. The sounds of sheep and horses filled my ear.

I pulled quietly on the old barn door, and spoke in a low

whisper to warn any human or animal of my presence. The smell of oats, which were piled in a bay on the far end of the barn, met my nose. Memories of a young lady, hay lofts, and short Coke bottles spinning wildly, mingled in my present thoughts. The dusty oats caused a coating of hazy dust to stream across the path of sunlight. Several cats scattered out an opening in the side of the barn. I ascended to the loft up an ancient ladder, wondering if it would crumble under me. A horse grunted and ground its teeth in an old plastic yellow bucket. Someone was near.

Through an opening in the loft I saw khaki-green pasture rolling out against the splendor of the surrounding mountains. The entire valley was surrounded by God's beauty. Large disks of hay in the shape of shredded wheat biscuits dotted the greening landscape.

I sketched out a floor plan for my dream barn on a notepad, imagining it full of rooms to hold human animals within. But I knew that my intentions in the barn could be misconstrued—that I was trespassing on someone else's life. I imagined encountering a codgy farmer with a long-barreled shotgun—someone I had no desire to confront! I slipped out the back door of the barn and walked back to the aspen-lined path above the valley. I found a grove of gold leaves and sat underneath in the warm dappled sunlight. I felt inspired to write and to meditate.

After a time, I walked back to the road, collected my motorcycle, and followed the two-lane highway through the mountains, taking in all the splendor of an autumn in the Rockies. As I turned down the highway, I came upon the familiar sight of an old general store—one where life steps back about fifty years and the interior is as though it had been borrowed from a set for *The Waltons* or *Little House on the Prairie*. I opened the screen door and walked into the dusty but lovely little shop. A cheerful older woman sat behind the counter knitting an afghan blanket. I stepped over to a Coca-Cola machine and plugged in my quarters, then took a seat on an old rocking chair in the front of the store.

The sound of men's voices grumbling something at the side of the store awakened me from my trance. I watched with great curiosity as they shuffled up into their meeting place at the front of the store on the clapboard porch. Three little old men shuffled past me to claim their "turf." I nodded, and they all returned the nod. They settled into their places—obviously there was no question as to whose chair was whose—and in an almost comical way, reached for their breast pockets and pulled out long, thick, pungent Churchill-length cigars. I wondered how many times this routine had been repeated over the years. There was such an obvious bond between the men that I held a sense of envy. I thought of my own good friends and wished that they had joined me on this motorcycle journey.

I moved my chair closer, slowly, so that I could enjoy the conversation of the salty threesome. I learned that for the past twenty years they had been coming down to Brown's Country Store to sit and drink their coffee black, smoke a cigar, and play games of checkers and cards. They commented on the latest installment of the newspaper's tales of

woe and expressed sorrow that the world of today had replaced the dreamy landscapes of the easier times when they
were young and ruled the world. They bounced around old
war stories and tales of conquest, of loves past. I wondered
how many times the same tales had been told and wished that
I were old enough to relate to the world when it seemed more
innocent and easy.

Near the spot where we sat was a large grove of aspen
trees. The tall trees reached up as though they could touch
the clouds that hung weakly in the thin blue autumn sky.
Their trunks were thick with many rings of years past, towering proudly over everything below. I thought of how aspens
become noticed and appreciated most when nearing the end
of their "life" each year. It is after a long summer season that
the cool air begins to touch their leaves, changing them forever. It is through the dying away that their beauty is recognized. Their long life of greenery yields to a later wisdom of
colors.

A wind picked up, and thousands of golden leaves flowed
from the aspens. The three men paused in their activity and
watched the heralding of another autumn in their mountains.

As I rode my motorcycle down the mountains to the
plains and home, I took in the show of the aspens dotting
through otherwise greened mountains. I thought of my wife's
grandfather and of how he loved to tell stories of the old
days on the railroad. How many more tales he must have had,
if I had simply sat still long enough to rock with him in his
back yard garden.

Taraxacum officinale Weber

BOTANICAL NAME

Dandelion

COMMON NAME

The dandelion is part of the chicory tribe, the aster family. Originally intro-
duced from Europe, it is a perennial that reproduces by seed that comes from
the flower. As the dandelion matures, it forms a white, fluffy seed ball. The
dandelion produces a milky, bitter juice that boasts of many medicinal prop-
erties. The serrated leaves form a small bushy plant, and from within, bright
golden flowers sprout. Being very hardy, dandelions grow naturally in
meadows, lawns, fields, and just about anywhere possible.

For many years I have dutifully tried to eradicate these in-
sidious weeds from my lawn. Even though the bouquets
of dandelion flowers my sons invariably present to my wife
are pretty, I have been bent on achieving a more perfect lawn.
Still, I live with a woman who believes in and uses herbs and
natural remedies. She cultivates the dandelions in the same
way that I cultivate vegetables from the garden. She has used
dandelions in some cures and, to my amazement, they do indeed work. Transplanted from the airborne seeds of meadows possibly miles away, dandelions have now been adopted
into the topology of my yard. Sooner or later my wife will
ask me to plant them purposely, I am sure.

As I RETREATED near a cozy fire in my den and set aside time to write, my mind wandered back to one of the last warm morning runs at the onset of autumn that I took with Snickers. As we passed through a valley, the sun was rising low to the east, casting a long ray of gold across the field. Snickers jogged ahead and passed a large patch of dandelions. As she passed, the wind from her body caused a stir. The globes of downy white seed lifted and meandered with a soft current of breeze upward. I stopped and watched the little parachutes, contemplating where the seeds might blow and start anew.

The dandelion is designed to depart from its place of origin, to float above the earth in search of an adopted home. Its seeds waft silently, borne on light breezes, until they "parachute" to the earth and set up home in their new environment. Dandelions form a strong taproot wherever their seeds rest and then germinate. Even domesticated weeds, if transplanted into an environment where they are nurtured and cared for, will often flourish and blend in well with the other common border garden varieties.

I remember the first time I looked into the face of my older son: it was the first time I was able to address a blood relative. His was the first face that I ever looked into that held any resemblance to mine. As a child, the only thing about my adoption that I seemed to obsess about was that I had no idea if my birth mother and natural father had the same features as me. If I were to see my natural parents in a grocery store, would I know it was them? Would it be like looking into a hazy mirror?

My adoptive father and his brothers and sisters all shared the same nose, a prominent feature within their bloodline. My nose didn't resemble theirs at all. When I looked at my friends next to their parents, I could see the physical similarities. So when I was young I would stand at the mirror, contorting my face, vainly imagining it as an adult's. Once I dusted flour at my temples, to help me envision the looks of my natural father. Yet somehow, even then, I knew that regardless of the lack of shared physical characteristics between my adoptive parents and me, there was a bond between us that surpassed the need for a common bloodline.

Character is a blending of genetics and environment. In personality and traits I am much like the father and mother who raised me, even though we share no blood. In numerous ways I became a "chip off the old block," like anyone raised by their biological parents. Although people who are adopted cannot look into the mirror and physically see that they are "becoming their parents," they can perceive that they are through their actions, deeds, and personality traits.

I and all the others who have been adopted into another family are like the flowers or weeds that were cultivated in one place and then placed in a garden separate from the intended one, flourishing or surviving there, as though destined to be there from the beginning. Like the dandelion, we form a strong "taproot" attachment to the environment in which we have been placed. The dandelion in its natural environment often relies on only the surface nutrients of the soil to sustain it; when it finds a home in the yard of a caring gardener, it takes a firmer, deeper root because of the care that the gardener shows the soil.

Nurture versus nature. Adopted persons wrestle with the issue many times over regarding their own foundation, their roots, the question of who they are. There were some low points in my life when I reflected negatively on my own origin. This happened once when I was rejected by a young woman I cared a lot for at the time; again, when shunned by a clique that at the time seemed so important to gain acceptance from; and again, during a time when my relationship with my adoptive father and mother was strained. All these times brought me to reflect upon my earliest "rejection," the rejection by my own natural parents. I felt like a weed, cast away from the rest of the garden, unlovely or somehow not good enough to stay with the rest.

What seems natural is that a child be raised, loved, and nurtured by the people who genetically brought it into this world. But I have come to recognize that, in reality, the authentic parents are the ones who comfort through frightening nights, referee sibling rivalries, nurture through life's difficulties and joys, and personify themselves to the child.

Being now a parent, I find it increasingly difficult to understand how a natural parent of a child could be so selfless as to release the child within her womb to another family. It is a wonderful thing to do, to endure the sacrifice and changes in her own life in order to gift other people who are unable to have their own children. The Bible says that God knows the number of hairs upon our head, that He knew us before the origin of the earth. That He knew us while we were still within the womb. If so, then He knew that we who have been adopted into other homes would form a link that is often stronger than genetics or bloodlines; it was part of His master plan, and many of us are the fortunate beneficiaries.

Often weeds make the most beautiful showing on earth. In fact, all the current plantings in gardens everywhere originated in natural settings and have been modified to fit in with a specific gardener's scheme. Some of the natural flowers, or "weeds," that I have placed in my gardens include wild columbine, wild strawberry, asparagus, mint, daisies, flax, and succulents. The adaptation is marvelous; one would hardly know that they weren't intended for my suburban garden originally.

The dandelion seeds that spread over miles of land to new meadows and places within which they can flourish symbolize to another the power of a transplanted soul. Often it is these "transplanted flowers" that flourish best if loved and nurtured, no matter whose hand it is by.

Though most often we think of the dandelion as a bothersome, unwanted weed, it is from dandelion flowers that we may drink sweet dandelion wine and view some of the earliest color in spring.

Ilex x meserveae

BOTANICAL NAME

Blue Holly

COMMON NAME

The holly prefers well-drained acidic soil and will tolerate either partial shade or full sun. In colder climates it is best to plant holly against a house or to protect it in some other way from windy conditions. A male and a female plant are required to produce beautiful red berries. The fruit as well as the leaves will hug the plant during autumn and winter months, providing beautiful variety to dormant beds. The holly will attract birds in search of berries. To ensure new growth and to maintain a low, bushlike growth, prune from the tips of the holly. You can prune the holly to a "tree shape" if preferred. The greenish-blue leaves offer a pretty, glossy effect to borders and a contrasting color for yards.

During the warmer months hollies almost become invisible—blending in as part of the landscape. But when winter silences most of the other surrounding growth, hollies become a focal point in the yard. Upon moving into a new house years ago, my wife and I were presented with three blue holly bushes to adorn the front of the white painted porch. On the coldest winter days the holly brought a colorful contrast to an otherwise monotone and sterile scenery about the house. Holly is always a reminder to me of the magical holiday season.

WINTER IS COMING. The delicate yellow flowers that sprang up along the holly bushes last spring, beckoning forth the red berries, are a long-ago memory. In autumn and winter, the holly bushes stick up through the snow, their red and green glossed leaves providing a stark contrast to the surrounding barren land. The holly bushes, along with the evergreen varieties, stand out in their attempt to beautify a landscape otherwise depressing, lonely, and stark at this time of year. They are like the people and events that provide hope in the midst of otherwise bleak circumstances.

Longingly I look to the garden, but it is seemingly empty earth, covered with only the first substantial snow of the autumn. The wind whistles through leaves that are trying with all their strength to cling fast to the trees that scratch against my window. These leaves are unwilling to fall or be blown from the life they have known, desperately clinging to the chance that maybe the sun will once more warm their tree trunks and allow them to grow green again. When they do inevitably float back to the earth from which they have sprung, they are renewed and become mulch of the future for the new generations to follow. Such is the cycle of life, the continuation of life from generation to generation.

When the gardens outside my windows grow silent and

dormant, anticipating the next season of birth and renewal, it is the time for me to draw inward and reflect, to relax and to remember. The easing away of autumn allows all living things to slow down and retreat inward, to find protection and hibernate against the elements that bring death if left exposed. Winter provides a time to wind down, to reflect and to draw inward the lessons of the previous clutter of activity, a time to cultivate the lessons of the warmer months. One of the favorite rooms in my house for me to while away time is my den, my "cave." It is where I am inspired to create and bring forth the reflections of this book.

It is now late, past midnight, and the children, my wife, and the dog have been asleep for hours. The house is silent, save for the few creaks from the awakening furnace and my fingers clacking along the keyboard. A soft, acoustical musical piece that I selected spins a mellow mood in the dark night. The music inspires me to reflect on childhood evenings, when I would awaken to the soft tones of the old phonograph spinning forth a gentle classical piece of music as my father sat in solitude at his desk or at the old kitchen table. Sometimes I would sneak from my bedroom and spy on my father, who would sit in the solitude of the sleeping house in the early hours of the morning. Blue-gray smoke would curl from his cigarette, haloing his head as he would sip from his coffee and work on a current manuscript or grade papers for his university classes. These early morning hours that he shared with no one cloaked him in mystery to me. I realize that in ways I have embraced his method of finding a quiet time and place to work, and as I get older I, too, lean toward the night hours when the activity of my children is confined to their dreams and the household is still.

We learn much from simple observation—and especially from our parents. My own parents had managed to instill in me—a creative, rebellious type—a sense of the times when it was necessary for me to conform to get along in this world. They also taught me to be gracious in the way I dealt with people. Now I find myself anxious that everything I do and say is being recorded on "tapes" within my own children's heads! Indeed, both my boys recently have been reaching out to me, yearning to spend time with me and pull me from my self-centeredness. At times their behavior borders on obnoxious, and it seems to be purposeful, a means to gain my attention. I remember doing this when I was a child as well.

I'd do just about anything to get noticed by my parents—even if what I received was negative feedback. There was a period of my childhood when I was in fourth grade and attending a Catholic school. We would arrive at school a half hour before classes were to begin so that we would have time to pay homage to God in the beautiful sanctuary of the oldest and largest church in my hometown. I recall the sights, sounds, and feeling I got when I sat in the old hardwood pews and gazed about at the magnitude of it all. The Stations of the Cross were in marble, and there were candles all about. Mysterious men in robes would silently scurry about, and on rare occasions incense smoked the whole place with an ancient rich smell that I thought must have smelled like Heaven.

About this time, my parents discovered that my brother

had a debilitating learning disorder that no one knew much about at this stage and that would require a lot of attention on both my parents' part. Academics had always come naturally to me, but as my parents began working with my brother, soon I started getting into trouble in class. I was gifted with the traditional ruler-across-the-knuckles on a few occasions for my fidgeting and acting up. After futilely struggling for authority with a solemn-faced sister dressed in the traditional black-and-white garb of The Flying Nun, I was banished to the rear of the classroom. My grades began to slip, and my behavior became less rambunctious and more subdued and depressed.

The straw broke after several schoolyard fights and minor rule infractions. One infamous morning in the half hour between church and school, the monsignor came upon me on the back steps of the church, drinking directly from the vessel of holy water intended for the dipping of one's finger and then crossing oneself in reverence to the Lord. I was immediately taken to Mother Superior's office, and my mother was called. I had been dealing with a lot of guilt over the anguish that I was causing by my acting out, and even if I wanted to stop doing the mischievous things I was doing, I wasn't sure I could. I figured that if you dabbed a bit of holy water on your forehead and received a blessing, think how much more internally blessed and cleansed I would be if I drank a whole cistern of it!

After a lot of one-on-one time with my mother, she realized the real reason for my attention-getting ploys was the fact that my brother was garnering so much attention and my academic prowess was being taken for granted. So why try?

She also found that I was having trouble seeing. She noticed that I would squint when viewing objects at a distance. A week later I was wearing ugly thick black plastic-framed glasses with thick lenses; for the first time in my life I could see the blackboard at the front of the class. I realized that the individual leaves on the trees didn't become a mass of color when you weren't holding them in your hand. That things remained in clear view even if you weren't right next to them.

Shortly after, my parents, realizing that I was not one to flourish under the many rules and regulations of parochial school, allowed me to enroll in a school with more liberal teaching methods. I no longer felt the need to flinch whenever I saw one of those wooden rulers with the metal edge, which always seemed to nick the bone on my wrist. My interest in school returned, and I won a few awards for my compositions and began reading voraciously.

The other thing that my parents in their sage wisdom began to do was to have me read with my brother, to become a part of his special education and to share what I knew with him in a nonthreatening way. When he experienced a victory in his reading, I was there with him, enjoying it and not simply feeling envious that my parents were fawning over him for something that just came naturally to me.

I thought of my own children now, with their talents and gifts, each very different from one another. Do I offer them the same kind of wisdom my parents had shown to me, so that a relationship between family members can flourish and they can enjoy selflessly all of our family's victories?

When I had tucked my older son into bed earlier that night, adding yet another warm blanket to his bed to protect against the cold, he had asked me what his mommy and I had been talking about during the day and why I seemed so sad. I had been deliberating over a difficult issue, and it was clouding what could otherwise be a terrific time for me. Although my wife and I had agreed not to burden our children with "adult worries," my son had picked up on my mood and realized that something was troubling me. With all of his nine years of wisdom and insight, he offered some very simple words to comfort me: "Daddy, remember that everything in life happens for a reason; someday you will understand what the reason is." His little arms reached around my neck and he squeezed tightly, showing me the depth of his love and understanding. I reeled back, astonished at the words coming from his lips. And I learned. His positive outlook and words eased my burden and allowed me to see that the issue I was confronting held less importance than I thought.

In fact, my son has always been a sensitive and intuitive child with a huge heart. At only three years of age he cried after seeing a documentary about pollution on television. My wife and I questioned him as to what it was that had saddened him so. His response was that people were killing "God's nature," and that someday he would keep people from throwing trash into the oceans and littering.

Another experience brought home to him the preciousness of every day. This was after he had spent several tense and scared nights in an oxygen tent for a dangerous bronchial condition. As he recovered, he watched another small boy, who was in the hospital with a serious injury. Putting aside thoughts of his own condition, he asked if it would be okay if he went over to the boy. Then he knelt down and prayed for the small, sleeping child: my son's mother's compassionate spirit and kindness had been passed on to the next generation. To this day he is resolved to complete his early mission of changing the world's view about our limited resources and holds a special place in his young heart for the underdog.

I wish that my mother could have been here to know my children and to be known by them. My older son is so much like her in many ways: eccentric in dress and taste, spirited and wondrous of the creation in which he lives. She would have loved him dearly, and yet I know that she does. For with the knowledge of her presence and the belief that she is closer than one might think, I realize that she is involved in my children's lives still, and knows them. Indeed, I can think of no better guardian angel for my children than my mother.

When I think about the way my son views the world—with uncommon regard—I am reminded that even in the hardest times there is growth, there is beauty to reflect upon. That the whole cycle of warmth and renewal will return, and that in the spring there will again be holly berries to attract the birds. My son was right: everything does indeed have a reason; it's just not always evident during the winter season.

Pumpkin

Dwarf Apple Tree

Washington Hawthorne

Scarlet Maple

Red-twig Dogwood

Aspen

Dandelion

Blue Holly

White Fir

Christmas-Rose

Spring Snowflake

Chinese Chestnut

Angel's Trumpet

Yesterday, Today, Tomorrow

A THANKSGIVING POEM

There's something about a fellow,
When he sees the harvest in
When the cows are in the stanchion.
And the grain is in the bin,
And the snow in furry curls,
In great clouds around the house,
Makes a grateful feeling in his being
As Thanksgiving's drawing near.

There's something in these features
When the cold north wind doth blow,
Makes the spirit of Thanksgiving
Within his swelling heart to glow,
Then he gathers in his neighbors,
And a feast he does prepare;
And for blessings, there's thanksgiving,
As they lift their hearts in prayer.

—Lionel A. Matott

Abies concolor

BOTANICAL NAME

White Fir

COMMON NAME

Native to Southern California and to Colorado, the white fir tolerates numerous soil conditions and doesn't require much water. If you want to enjoy the medium-growing fir, plant from balled and burlaped trees from a nursery. You can plant young seedlings from bare root. Ready your soil with sandy loam and compost and allow for full sun. Allow ample space for an eventual fifty feet of height and a wide base that tapers to a conical top. The white fir is a lovely addition to any yard. It is not only pretty but is a home to some: within one of the fir trees in my yard I have counted three bird's nests.

The white fir, as well as its cousin, the Fraser fir, and the pine tree, makes for a classic Christmas tree.

As a child, my enjoyment of the Christmas tree was, unfortunately, short-lived. My mother was a stickler for tradition when it came to the holidays, and in her European ancestry the tree was brought in just before the Christmas celebration. My father, also a stickler and not particularly into the holidays, had his own tradition: New Year's Day marked the end of the tree. He looked forward to the tree's coming down with great anticipation and the whole business being over. My wife and I now let the tree into the house right after Thanksgiving, and if it doesn't come down in the first week of January . . . well, that is just the way it goes.

ONE NIGHT YEARS AGO as I sat near the soft white glow of the string of minute lights on the fir tree in the living room and felt the warmth of the fire in the fireplace as its radiance reached into the otherwise darkened room, I had what might best be described as a minor epiphany. I could not believe what had happened to me, the ultimate Christmas lover. I, who had insisted for years that my wife stay up late with me watching all the sentimental movies and who had always loved every moment of the holidays. I, who had consciously decided years ago that I would never dread the holidays the way my father had every year, or tarnish the meaning of the holidays for my own children. Somehow I had become Ebeneezer Scrooge, the self-centered man who had to be shaken up and brought back to things of importance.

The sun had begun to set, and the house was somewhat dark on Christmas Eve. I had been furiously working in the den to finish a business project while my wife visited with her sister in the kitchen. My children played gleefully and loudly in the basement with their cousins in anticipation of the coming festivities. The Christmas tree cast an eerie glow across the room as the TV spouted out the referee's call against the opposing football team: our home team boys were putting the other team away in the second half, dashing the other team's playoff dreams. For me, this Christmas Eve game was long awaited, but now I was more intent on the computer and the deadline that lay before me. If my family and I were going to enjoy future Christmases in comfort, I would need to sacrifice now.

I heard someone moving around in the room but was far too busy to look up. "Daddy, did you know that the geese fly south every year?" Ethan, my younger son, stood at the window watching a large, V-shaped flock overhead. All day the geese had been flying westward over our neighborhood, honking and fussing as the cold wind nipped at them. I briefly felt a sense of envy that they knew exactly where they were going, knew the purpose of their journey. There was no moral dilemma about the path they were taking; they were simply following instinct.

"Uh-huh," I grunted, returning my gaze to the computer after flashing a quick glance at the TV to see if the score was displayed.

"Daddy, do you think the geese are flying south to see their grandmas and grandpas for Christmas?" my son called out to me from the kitchen. The children had now joined my wife and her sister in the kitchen to "help" in the baking process and to decorate the Christmas cookies. "DAD?!"

I moved to stuff the Sunday paper into the fireplace under the grate and ignite the fire for the traditional Christmas Eve festivities. From the flue in the fireplace, I heard the soft, constant barking of the geese that flew overhead. My son's voice seemed a distant echo, and I figured at some point my wife would answer him.

"Hmmm?" I halfheartedly responded.

"Dad, did you hear me?"

"What?" Impatiently I pushed back to the table in front of the football game that I was not paying any attention to. My computer blinked onto the screen saver and seemed to call to me to come back. I needed to find out more to complete the proposal that was due the day after Christmas. What a hassle to have all of the critical people around me at the office out for the holidays! I needed to finish the year strong, yet I couldn't in good conscience call upon my support team on Christmas Eve. It would be necessary for me to work on the project after the children went to bed. I also would have to stay up late to do my Santa duties—Lord knew he needed help!

"Dad, how come you don't hear me?" My son stood at the end of the leather couch.

I was way behind at work and somewhat annoyed that I was given the tasks of fire starter and other festive jobs that didn't seem to hold the same importance as the work that would provide the toys that my children wanted for Christmas. "I heard you."

"So, *do* they?"

"I'm sorry, do they what?"

My little boy looked at me in exasperation. "Do the geese go to their grandparents' houses or no?"

"I am sure they do," I halfheartedly replied.

He rolled his eyes and several moments later I heard him in the kitchen asking his mother the same question that he had just asked me. I went on about my work.

That evening my family and I opened our hand-picked Christmas Eve presents. I felt somewhat smug that the children had been so excited by the gift choices; after all, I had been the provider of the bounty. My wife helped the children carry their loot to their rooms and tucked them into bed, while I tried to get a little research done on the proposal so that I wouldn't have to be up all night and then be exhausted the next day at my in-laws for the Christmas festivities. Besides, my wife and I still had the tradition of the Christmas movie ahead as we wrapped and placed the Christmas Day presents beneath the tree.

We wrapped the remaining gifts and laid the stockings out on the hearth, full of goodies. My wife fell asleep with a peaceful look on her face right after old Scrooge, in the movie *A Christmas Carol*, found the knocker resembling Marley. Something about the peace on my wife's face caused a twinge deep within me. I looked long and hard at the beautiful woman whom I had loved for so many years, a woman who has become as much a part of me as my own flesh. A memory flashed across my mind, a time when we were first in love. It was a Christmas many years before, when all I could think about was being with her, sharing my holiday in a meaningful and poignant way with her. A year when her father took me, then her boyfriend, with him to select a Christmas tree.

Suddenly I saw on the screen the look of the girlfriend of Scrooge—her turning from him because he had forgotten the meaning of love and had replaced her with this new lover: prosperity and money. I shook the look off, dismissing it as sentimental reasoning, but then remembered a poem that I had read halfheartedly to the kids the night before, about sugarplums dancing through their heads. Then I thought of the serenity that my wife was enjoying as my stomach continued to tighten each hour that passed while I was not finishing the business proposal that would ensure my family a bountiful Christmas the next year.

I sat and watched, mesmerized. Finally, Scrooge danced around his room with a new spirit and made good on all of his past wrongs. The movie's moral and spiritual conclusion reminded me of George Bailey holding ZuZu in his arms as his friends gathered around him at the end of *It's a Wonderful Life*, a testimony to what is real in life. Of the little girl in *Miracle on 34th Street* who had everything she wanted except for a family, and of Bing Crosby and Marjorie Reynolds at the end of *Holiday Inn* as they discovered the true meaning of Christmas in their love for each other.

Why was I being haunted by all of these sentimental

scenes and thoughts? As my computer lay next to me I sipped from a cooling snifter of brandy and decided that I would make more of an effort the next morning to give my kids some attention before I turned to my work. Maybe I would set aside an hour to build something out of their new Legos or throw a ball with my little sportsmen, who now understood and loved the games of football, basketball, and baseball as well as any sports buff twice their age. Then they would certainly understand my need later on to go to the office for a few hours to pick up some information to complete the proposal. No one would be in the office on Christmas, providing me with a perfect opportunity to get something done. I stopped the video and headed into the kitchen to get a glass of eggnog. The refrigerator light shone into the family room and caught a large white envelope that had been placed in the lit tree. Sure that my wife had cheated on our "no gift" policy, I walked in and removed it from the tree; curiosity had gotten the best of me.

It was addressed simply "FOR SANTA ONLY." It was in my younger son's handwriting, and I knew that I should read it: it probably required a response. The letter was simple and sweet. As I read it through, I felt a pang of remorse as I realized that my son had asked me how to spell several words in the letter earlier that morning, but I had sent him off to see his mother, certain that what *I* was working on had more relevance than the words *he* was struggling with, and that my wife was *just* baking cookies.

Dear Santa,

Thaks for all of the presants lost year, the
bike is redly cool, bout my Daddy keeps promising
to ride with me, never does. He told me
that he wowd raise the seet better. My
mommy tried but he used the wrong tool and
it still twists. This year I want my daddy
to get the week off so we can thro the
football restle like we used to.

Love, Ethean.

As I finished the letter, I felt my stomach thud.

Tears flooded my eyes and dropped onto the crayoned page. Echoing in my mind were my son's earlier questions: "Daddy, how do you spell 'Daddy'?" "How do you spell 'throw'?" "How do you spell 'bicycle'?" I remember thinking that he was awfully ungrateful to ask for another bicycle— after all, last year he had gotten a perfectly good bicycle, and it should still be in good condition.

I walked into my office and typed a memo to my boss stating that the remaining project would have to wait due to some pressing family issues. Then I turned off the computer and vowed that I would not turn it back on until the second week in January. I climbed the stairs to my sons' bedrooms and entered quietly. My younger son, restless and wakeful in anticipation of Santa Claus's arrival, rolled over to me. I knelt beside his bed and thanked God for the gift of my son.

Ethan sensed that something was wrong and asked me if I was okay. I whispered into his ear that I loved him and that the geese were arriving at their grandparents' houses in the South in time for Christmas dinner. He smiled and hugged me around the neck, then rolled over to find his own sugarplum fairies.

I spent the next week wrestling with my sons, spending time just being boys, and remembering why my wife and I had married and decided to have children.

Perched on the boughs of the Christmas fir tree we put up in the family room is an ornament given to us the year that Ethan was born. It depicts a family of four, smiling.

Helleborus niger

CLASSIFICATION

Christmas-Rose

COMMON NAME

The Christmas-rose is native to Europe and will grow to heights of six to twelve inches. It prefers moist, well-composted soil in partial shade, and provides winter and spring flowering. Propagated by seed and root division, it produces white flowers with a yellow center and burgundy freckles and thick leaves. The flowers change to green with age. The Christmas-rose is good for use in woodland gardens, rock gardens, and mixed borders and beds. It looks spectacular against a cedar-mulched bed.

My mother was like the Christmas-rose native to Europe. She was a transplanted European fully American—like the German traditional Christmas carol *"Es ist ein Rose entsprungen,"* or "Lo, How a Rose E'er Blooming." She was like the rose in many ways: her outward petals to many seemed brash and forward in their color, but what she held in her heart was the pure white of the Christmas-rose. The capability to love people beyond most narrow constraints was one of the things that her friends remember most fondly about her. She was indeed like a rose, with beautiful and unique scents, yet thorny if you touched upon the wrong part.

WHEN MY MOTHER AND I TOOK PHOTOGRAPHS, she usually insisted on including the climbing rose on our house's outside chimney as a backdrop. We shared a lot of time together, just she and I. We enjoyed each other's company, and it seemed that we were friends long before most people find a unique "friendship" with their parents. As a young woman, she had raised her younger brothers and sisters, and so had learned much about what was important to belabor and what would simply work its way out.

She rarely sweated the small stuff; when I was young and asked her if I could get my ear pierced, she said, "It's your ear. Why are you asking me? By the way, it hurts like hell, so make sure you take a lot of aspirin after you do it." I waited for about four more years before I finally did pierce it, and she was right: it did hurt. When I told her that I was thinking of smoking marijuana with some of my friends, she remarked that it was one thing she had always been curious about as well, and would I mind bringing some home to her to try with me as well. I was too embarrassed to do so, and so I didn't bother with it at the time either. When I decided that I should run away from home, she asked me to make sure that I took some warm clothes and then asked me if I would be home in time for dinner or not. I did and I was. But when

I told her in my turbulent teenage years that I had considered suicide as an alternative to the issues I was dealing with, she told me she loved me and would die of a broken heart if I even considered it further. I cried and she held me and we talked deep into the night, until the problem that seemed so large at the time diminished into its true relevance.

She was a darn good friend. As a young child, I called her "Mommy" until I realized that all my friends called their mothers "Mom," so I called her that and then I called her "Julie" when I felt that I was all grown up and that we had reached a level of equals. She didn't mind because it was clear to both of us that she would always be Mom. The night that she died as I held her hand in mine; I called her "Mommy" again, and missed her immediately.

There was one very magical holiday season in my life, a time of innocence before the corruption of the world was able to penetrate my childhood. That Christmas season would be my last with Santa. The last that I would sit in wonder at the fireplace and marvel at how the huge man was able to fit with all my presents. The last time I would look upon the illustrations of Grandma Moses in the book *The Night Before Christmas* and envision Santa and the reindeer atop our house exactly the way she had depicted them so brilliantly.

My mother took me with her to a very elegant restaurant in the large city south of our small town, my reward for tagging along with her on a shopping trip. It was Christmas time and the lights on the great Christmas trees shone beautiful colors across the darkening streets. On the top of one of

the skyscrapers there was a towering batch of wrapped presents. The whole city seemed to be in total celebration, the
streets wet with falling snow, cars and people bustling about
with the season on their minds. I held my mother's hand and
packages as we went into one elegant store after another, mesmerized with the escalators and the smell of wet wool and
leather gloves as we made our way through the crowds. Santa
Claus stood at the front of the stores, and the bells from the
Salvation Army ringers punctuated the air and drowned out
some of the traffic noise.

People hurried in and out of stores with great bundles of
packages. My mother held my hand in hers and was warmed by
the comments that people would make to her about her little
boy. I remember looking up at her and thinking that she was
the most wonderful woman. She was always in such control,
and would navigate the strange city streets as though she lived
there. She met people with such enthusiasm and confidence.

After a morning of shopping and several return trips to
the car to unload the pile of presents, we entered a fancy
restaurant and were met by a finely dressed maitre d' who
teased me about having a cocktail before my meal. A smoky,
wonderful smell filled the place, mixing with the savory foods
and my mother's Chanel No. 5, which I gave her every year
for Christmas, with a little (a lot of, actually) help from my
father.

I remember the tinkling of Christmas music that was
playing as my mother and I sat on the top floor of one of the
taller buildings in the city, looking out to the majestic Rocky

Mountains as the snow fell onto the street far below. I remember feeling so safe with her there, so important. I was her date at an elegant restaurant, dressed in a little suit and a woolen coat, just like the one that John John Kennedy wore years earlier. The music—"Chestnuts roasting on an open fire"—played with a jazzy beat. The voice was dreamy and spoke of the holiday magic afoot.

The napkins were of fine material, and the starch felt good in my hands. The mood, set by the silver settings, fine linens, lit candles, and a beautiful arrangement of roses, was in stark contrast to the winter cold that gripped the outside. A roaring fireplace warmed the entire restaurant, and the fine silver globes that the waiters carried about, filled with delicious steaming dishes that smelled of rich gravy and sumptuous broth, clinked in a glorious symphony of hustle and bustle. I was used to gourmet cooking and knew a lot of the offerings on the elegant menu. I pleased my mother when I asked the waiter questions, using the proper French pronunciation that I had heard so many times used in my home (French often being the secret language of my parents when speaking of things not intended for my ears).

When the waiter brought an elegant silver tray to the table loaded with various sweet delights, my eye was caught by all that was chocolate. Instead, my mother enticed me to share with her a favorite dessert from the tradition of the English. It was the first time that I ever had bread pudding. The thought of pudding and bread didn't sound good to me, but when they served the rum-flavored bread pudding, I thought

I would never taste anything so delightful again. We ate it with fine vanilla ice cream, two spoons sharing a dessert after a perfect meal. She also let me have a small coffee of my own. I felt so grown up. The holidays began to sing their way into my heart in a magical new way that I still remember with much fondness.

Later, we went to see a production of *The Nutcracker*. My mother mentioned that I shared with Tchaikovsky my middle name, Peter; possibly someday I, too, would write beautiful music. Even though we lived in a rural area, my mother, a New Yorker at heart, wanted me to be exposed to the arts that she relished. The swirling of the Arabians in dance, the Chinese, and then of course the Sugar Plum Fairy, were all a wonder and delight. The sights and sounds of the production seen through the eyes of this child were magical, and with my mother in her theater gloves and her enthusiasm this was a dear time in my life that engrained a true love for the arts and holiday season. As a child I would see many more plays and works of the theater with her and my father.

What I remember most about the trip was that she treated me as an equal; she spoke to me of things that were important to her. I was not yet a teenager and yet she spoke to me as though my opinions were important. She told me from as early as I can remember that I could be anything in the world that I wanted to be, that God had a very special task for me in life, and that to the best of her ability she would see to it that it was fulfilled.

I loved her so much; she was such a loving mother. Yet she also was a very hard mother to live with because her expectation of me was so high. I remember times when she would go out of her way to make my tasks harder just to see the character that would form as a result. As a parent, I now can understand what she was doing, but it took a long time for me to see what her plan had been. We had been so close when I was a child, but then experienced a great distance as I pulled away to independence as a teenager. She grew tougher on me when she saw that my independence was taking the wrong course, a task that was surely difficult for her. She remarked to me, to my shame at times, that she wondered where the sweet young boy had gone and who was this stranger to replace him. Even in my most rebellious times I took these loving comments to heart, and they literally saved me from doing some of the things that I otherwise would have done. I couldn't bear to go so far that I would hurt her that much.

The rebellion I was experiencing had begun when she was in the greatest throes of her first round with the brain tumor. I believe in some way I was shielding myself from the pain of watching her decline and not knowing how to help. When she had all but lost her reason because of the tumor that was growing undetected within her head, her doctor had told her that if she wanted to get rid of her headaches she should get rid of her stress. She asked him plainly, "Then do *you* want my kids?"

One thing that I always enjoyed about her was her deep

belief and confidence in the spiritual aspects of life. She had a close affinity with Mary, the mother of God. Many people pray to Mary, for she is an essential part of the Catholic faith, but my mother's reasoning for praying to Mary was unique—some might think it irreverent, but her intention was good. She would say that she preferred praying to Mary because Mary was a mother and had to deal with a unique son in the same way that my mother did. Now, I very much doubt that my mother thought of me in the same way that she did about Jesus, but she did say to me with some level of regularity that Jesus worried his mother when He went to the temple, and that Jesus followed His heart and His convictions to the point that his mother lost Him finally, breaking her heart totally. "Only a mother could understand the specific prayers of another mother."

Roses, a reminder of motherhood, are gathered and purchased by many, young and old, to revere those with a special place. The roses' thorns protect the blooms, and the essence of a rose can be recognized in any flower bed. *Es ist ein Rose entsprungen.* Roses are often a symbol of love and enduring respect. The scent of a rose draws people back to memories, as do many other sensory "events." The Christmas-rose draws me back to holiday's tinkling tunes, scented candles, pine sap, Christmas cookies, and a magical winter's day spent with a very special person.

AWAKENING SPRING

Awakening from her long winter's sleep,
Mother nature from her cover peeps;
Throws off her night-cap white and fair,
And pins pretty blossoms in her hair;
Then with her best green dresses on,
She hastens out to meet the meadow and pond;
Two of her children these seem to be,
For they leap in joy her face to see,
Then the forest, her full-grown child,
Pride of her heart, welcomed her smile
With a wave of green banners o'er her head,
And soft green mosses for her bed;
Then he asked his chorus for her to sing
And they sang their sweetest songs of spring.

—Lionel A. Matott

Leucojum vernum

BOTANICAL NAME

Spring Snowflake

COMMON NAME

The spring snowflake prefers moistened, well-drained, composted soil in partial shade. Fall planting is best for the bulbs, which should be planted two to three inches deep. They flower while snow is still imminent during the spring. They provide flowers in clumps and look similar to many crocus plantings. The petite and charming white flowers will grow to ten inches and hang their heads toward the ground; a yellow spot along the bonnet encompasses the entire flower. They cluster on diminutive, arching stems with narrow pointed leaves that look similar to grass. They are beautiful in wooded areas and shade gardens. When mixed in a border with the dwarf iris and other small bulb plantings, they truly are a winter-into-spring spectacle.

In the backyard of my boyhood home, spring meant splashes of color that pushed their way through the wakening soil. In our back yard, near the base of the large cottonwood tree that had stood for many decades, delicate spring flowers would arrive in clumps of glory. Among them were spring snowflakes, symbols of incredible resilience that heralded the warmth that was soon to come.

THE SNOW HAS BEEN SITTING uncharacteristically long on the ground, and the sun has held back from providing any warmth for some time now. The trees, though beautiful, appear forlorn, reaching and searching in vain for the sun, looking skeletal as they desperately mingle with the frosty surrounding air. It has been months since the bark felt the heating rays that warm the sap, causing the tree's vital juices to run to the extremities of the branches. It seems so long since the warmth of the sun and the earth allowed for the buds set in warmer days to burst with life and provide nourishing greens, reds, and burnished oranges, brown, and tans to paint the landscape.

Yet the soil is slowly awakening. Small signs of warmer days to come occur not long after Valentine's Day. The arms of the trees bear slight hints of impending buds. Soon, even as the snow is falling, the little spring snowflakes, crocuses, and hyacinths will pierce through the soil and bring hope back to gardeners restless behind glass windows. These delicate early plants testify to the will and ability to thrive, to the strength of life even when it is against the odds in a hostile environment.

I returned from jogging under the canopy of an ashen gray sky and reflected on the magical morning. There was an extraordinary thinness to the air, and I felt as though I was once again being prepared for an experience of illumination. This suspense heightened my awareness and made me take special note of my surroundings in the white, barren valley under the shadow of the great Rocky Mountains, allowing my mind to clear in anticipation of another gift possible from my Creator. The chill hit my nose, and I pulled my clothing tighter to my neck. Soon my body would warm against the elements, and I would enjoy the jog.

As I ran, I was amazed that for the entire time the sun was shining brightly from the east as large snowflakes feathered to the ground slowly. I reflected on the metaphor of the single snowflake, with its unique individuality. Each is crafted delicately in its own pattern and shape, formed in silence and under specific design. Each is unique in every way, able to differentiate itself from the masses. Yet some snowflakes are destined to become great and some to burn out before they even hit the ground. Most—although individual and beautiful in their own way—are destined to have little impact until combined with many others, becoming a part of a greater good. There are those that endure the test of time and become the basis for glaciers, adding great beauty to the world around them. Other flakes have a less grandiose purpose, but a very important short-lived purpose in their own right: a child's winter wonderland, where snow caves, snowmen, and snow sculptures may have been created, is composed of temporary and seemingly indistinct masses of flakes, which stamp an eternal memory in the mind of their possessor. A remembrance that will stay so that, when it is experienced again and again, something from a former time comes alive. Yet some snowflakes melt the moment they hit the inhospitable earth, not allowed to complete their intended journey here, for earth is too hazardous for their delicate nature and does not embrace their potential and contribution. These are the snowflakes that will return and be cultivated close to God in His garden.

Now huddled in the warmth of my home, with a fireplace at my back and bookshelves lined with volumes both read and still awaiting me, I meditate on the analogy of the single snowflakes and their often temporal impact. I think of a particular friend who lost his battle against the harsh ravages of disease, yet to the end showed beauty and a unique love for the simple beauties of life. A dear friend I knew since high school, someone I thought I knew well then yet only came to know after I tried to understand him later in our lives. He was a close friend in high school, and soon after we left the hallowed halls of our school I heard that he had gone to San Francisco. Shortly after, I found out that he was gay and had gone to escape the small-town attitude that would not have allowed him to flourish in that day and age. We drifted apart due to circumstances in our lives, our obvious differences, and my stilted understanding of the fact that he was still the very same person I had known and loved.

Ten years later, he and I "met" again at our high school reunion. The man I met then was no different in many ways to the boy-man I had known many years before, yet there were profound differences that I had yet to understand in his life. He wrestled with my son at the family picnic party. We drank beer and hung out just like old times. The second night of the reunion he decided that he could no longer take the shunning that he had been receiving from our old "friends." We went to a hangout that we had known many years before and sat on the roof of my car and talked through the night. As the night wore on, our friendship returned, stronger than it had ever been. He told me very honestly about his life partner and how difficult it was to live in a world of prejudice. He told me how hard it had been to lose many friends to relentless disease, how hard it had been to lose his own mother, and then, as the sun began to rise on the eastern horizon, he told me that he himself had been diagnosed with HIV. I suddenly felt the loss of the previous ten years quite painfully. As I realized that I was to lose him again, I grieved with him.

Soon after, he talked to me late into the night as he tried to help me adjust to the loss of my own mother. He listened, understood, and comforted me with his experience and words. We wrote and talked often, and he told me of his disease's progress. One summer, as my family drove down the road following the coast of northern California, we arrived in San Francisco with great anticipation. I had journeyed there to see him, for I had never met his life partner, had never seen his life there. We planned to surprise him. He had told me he was coming near the end of his life, and I wanted badly to see him one last time.

As we neared the area where he lived in San Francisco, I stopped within blocks of his house at a phone booth to let him know I was in town. Someone else answered his phone, a woman who told me that my friend and his partner had died two and three weeks before. I felt the air escape from my lungs and felt a deep hollowness and grief. I had lost a beautiful friend; the world was poorer for the loss. Several months later, his three sisters, his father, and many other friends and relatives came to my hometown. His sisters asked me to pick a place for his memorial service. We all sat up on the cliffs of a large lake where he and I had spent many carefree days of our youth jumping off of the cliffs into the water below; it was the same place that he and I had gone during the reunion. We said good-bye to him, a community of friends from all walks of life joined together by one wonderful person. He was like the resilient spring snowflake, short-lived and yet exquisite and impressive. Spring snowflakes show their strength by pushing their way into a hostile environment and thriving, not allowing the world around them to cause retreat but standing up against the odds and fighting to spread their beauty and return again for many years to come. He had imprinted so many people positively in his life; he lives on in the memory of many.

So the next time you hear that you don't stand a snow-ball's chance in Hell, remember that God recycles for future generations of precipitation. Plant some spring snowflakes and let them remind you to work to overcome the odds in your own circumstances.

Castanea mollissima

BOTANICAL NAME

Chinese Chestnut

COMMON NAME

The chestnut prefers well-drained loam and favors full sun. It can handle heat and drought well. It is nut bearing, disease resistant, and slow growing. However, the tree eventually will reach over forty feet in height, with bushy branches covered with pointed, serrated leaves that turn russet in autumn. In summer it will be covered with white flowers, which will be replaced with nuts in autumn. Smaller chestnut trees can be started from seed and bare-root seedlings.

One autumn, while in Paris with my wife, we strolled among many gardens and parks, taking picnic lunches of French bread, cheeses, and chocolate among the great plantings of flowers and towering trees. After ambling for a long stretch we noticed a very French-looking artist, complete with easel and beret, working with oil paints under a large chestnut tree. Street vendors stood near the famous museums with their roasters, selling chestnuts to tourists, the smell of the roasting delicacies a delight to the passing crowd. I picked up several chestnuts from the sidewalk and stuffed them into my pocket—perhaps to create a future tree many miles from where they were found.

IN A QUAINT LITTLE SHOP IN PARIS, my wife and I purchased a large loaf of dark, round French country bread dusted with fine flour; tangy sweet tomatoes; a large block of soft baby mozzarella cheese with a fresh sprig of basil; and some enormous chunks of rich, dark chocolate. We sat together on a bench watching the Parisians and tourists from all over the world stroll along the sidewalks, and for a moment, with the Arc de Triomphe at the head of the mall and the Louvre facing us in the park, felt at home. I fell in love with Paris, and I fell in love with my wife all over again in the wonderful city of amour. The bench on which we sat was surrounded by geraniums, scented so that when you brushed them, the air filled with the scent of lemons and floral perfumes, beckoning forth memories in the strange, haunting way the senses can.

During winter, the windows in my childhood home were filled with the bright colors of geraniums. My father placed geraniums in masses near the windows to capture the weak effort of the sun to warm them. All through even the harshest of winters we were reminded of the promise of spring and the coming blooms by his thoughtful plantings.

I noticed when my father was glad, he would hum-sing a sort of song. It was always the same: *La-da-deee, la-da-da.* My father would hum-sing when he studied the geraniums in the windows, so different from the winter wheat fields and otherwise barren landscape, silenced by winter's cold. The sight of the geraniums inspired his mind to drift to warmer times to come.

Today herb topiaries are domesticated in my house. They provide a gardening delight and a new winter hobby, one that is becoming a favorite indoor gardening pastime, a way to tide over my yearnings to putter with green things while the winter blankets the gardens. Quite similar in reason and focus to the ancient art of bonsai, the pruning of herbs is intended for quiet meditation, contemplation, and enjoyment. Herbs can be a miniature form of a topiary tree, and careful pruning assures that the shape and size desired are achieved.

The windows of my home are lined with rosemary, lemon verbena, sweet bay, and basil. The mixture of these scents, along with that of the scented geraniums, is as close to the smells of a summer garden as one can get on a cold wintry day. My childhood home's kitchen cabinets, too, were lined with every possible herb and seasoning that my mother could garner. She would deviate from recipes and create her own masterpieces. She took such delight in the enjoyment of food, respecting the herb's place as a seasoning. The resulting flavor would change the mundane into a pleasure, an event rather than simply a meal. The spices and her individual interpretation of recipes made such a difference, changing the ordinary to the extraordinary. In the same manner, people in many different shapes, sizes, and personalities add spice to life.

At one point in my adult life, my mother and I had a deep and meaningful conversation about relationships. She mentioned the good fortune I had had to marry into a family that accepted me, and that I should cherish my relationship with my wife's mother because she was "the salt of the earth." My mother and my mother-in-law were very different people with very different perspectives on life and the world, yet somehow they forged a nice relationship with each other, one with little regard for the competition that is likely in marriage situations.

Early on in my days of gardening my own piece of land, I was mentored by my wife's mother. I have never been comfortable with thinking of her as an "in-law." Now she is too dear for me to think of her as anything but my third mother. I say "third mother" because I was birthed by one mother, adopted and raised by a "real mother," and now am blessed with another mother. No one could ever replace any of the three of my mothers because each has had a unique reason for being a part of my life.

The first woman, who as I understand it met me only in passing but knew me to her core, as all mothers with unborn children in their wombs must, made a decision that required much character and a reverence for the life that she held. She, through magnanimous love, enabled people that were unable to have their own children to have a child after all. She is a blessed woman in my heart, and I will always love her for her gift to me of life.

The second woman that God gifted me with was my "real mother." Who else but a real mother would diaper, comfort, love, endure, and believe in me at those times when all evidence was that of failure? My mother was a complex friend, a loving parent, and a comrade through thick and thin. She is no longer alive in the traditional sense, but she is fully alive in my heart, mind, and spirit. She left an indelible imprint on my life in the same manner that every parent does with their children—and in that she lives on.

Then comes the third mother that God has blessed me with, my wife's mother. She has loved me as her own almost from the start. The first time I told her as a teenage college student that I would marry her daughter some day, she remarked simply, "Don't count your chickens till they hatch." As soon as she adjusted to the fact that I was becoming a permanent fixture in her house, and mostly her kitchen, she opened her home and her heart to me, and has become a very dear friend and my complicitor in the garden. For purposes of clarity, both yours and mine, she is called "NayNay." My older son, her oldest grandchild, named her that many years ago as he struggled to grasp the English language, and that is how I think of her. She is called to the table this way, so I will refer to her as NayNay from here on. NayNay has already left so huge an impact of positive love and adventure on my children that her legacy will grow and flourish through many years to come.

NayNay is a master gardener, and acts as a consultant to many of us gardeners who struggle with our lack of "plans" and our inability to make what we see on the cover of organic gardening and horticulture magazines our own. NayNay had always hoped that one of her children would take on her love of the soil; neither daughter ever did. Her only son loves to garden indoors but as he lives more than a thousand miles away, I am her "child" with a love of the rich soil and a desire to "paint" across the horticultural canvas. NayNay can grow things on concrete—no sun and no water needed. It seems she only has to look on a plant and it knows that it is loved and responds. In many ways she has provided the easel for my garden paintings.

"So what is your plan?" she would remark with a knowledgeable smirk on her face as she would look on my spring growth and immediately identify that I had made some huge error in calculations of size, shape, texture, and future appearance. She often would notice that I had planted everything in a haphazard way, that the plants that would grow three feet higher than those things behind them would have to be moved again so that the low, clinging plants would not remain unseen. After many years of moving the same plants around three or four times, I learned that if I invited her over for some iced tea or a sandwich before planting, I would get some consulting proactively, instead of a finger pointing and a feeling that she had taught me the same lesson several times before.

She would stretch my imagination to areas of the yard that I had not before considered. Now if I don't have a plan, I call her even before I visit the nursery. There also have been times when a plant or two has shown up mysteriously in a place that she mentioned needed something and to which I didn't attend in short order.

All of my friends and family are quite aware that if a plant is in need of rescue, I will take it on as a personal challenge. NayNay is the same way. One fall many years back, my wife and I had a house built—a medium-sized house in the country with a large yard. It was my effort to replicate my country childhood life for my own children. We moved into the house and immediately I saw a large job ahead of me. With few financial resources available after the house closing and the energy of youth, I decided to take on the landscaping of the large yard myself. The immediate need was for trees; we lived out on a prairie with blowing winds and miles of field behind the house. I would etch out a beautiful yard as well as provide a wind break so the dust on the windowsills wouldn't drive my citified wife back to the comforts of the city that she missed already. I would attempt to capture some of the free-flowing garden landscape that my father had created when I was a child. But NayNay and I needed to find a way to populate the yard with trees without populating my credit-card bill.

Another person of great relevance to both my life and this story is NayNay's life partner, my father-in-law. I regard him as a close friend and one of my counselors of life. His nickname incidentally is "Coda"; he calls me "Moots." I think he didn't know my last name for the first couple of years because he hoped I would go away; he did not realize that his daughter was trapped in love and destiny.

On my morning runs near NayNay and Coda's house I had noticed that there was a field with broken structures and lines of trees stretching for miles. I found it strange that an obviously neglected field had trees ranging in size from one to five feet tall. I asked NayNay what she made of it, and she let me know that she would do some investigation and get back with me. It turned out the trees were there because the old place used to be a nursery. It had been in disrepair for years, and so it probably would be okay to dig out some of the trees as they were destined to be replaced someday with tract homes or a strip mall. We decided to liberate as many as our truck would move. The first trip to the field, NayNay acted as the foreman while I dug and sweated trees out of the soil. Within an hour of beginning our task, a policeman pulled into the dirt road on a motorcycle and strutted up to us; we were caught red-handed with the goods. NayNay turned on the charm and explained to the gruff man that without nourishment and care the trees would wither and that there was enough there for all to share. Minutes later he asked if he were to come back the next day, could she help him decide what ones would work for his own yard. The agreement was made, and I almost expected him to pick up a shovel and assist us with our task. Only NayNay could have worked that out so well.

In short order, at NayNay's instruction and with a plan in hand, that weekend Coda and I went back to the field to work. Some of the trees lifted out of loam easily and some, with their roots reaching deep into the earth, cost us much sweat and back-breaking toil to lift them from the soil. We dug out some twenty trees: cottonless cottonwoods for fast growth, plum trees for reddish-purple color against the gray house, fast-growing Russian olive trees, and willow and locust trees to add interest to the yard. To finish it off we purchased a Nanking cherry tree, a blue spruce, ten aspen trees, and miles of sod. We transported hundreds, seemingly thousands, of perennials from nurseries and my father's and NayNay's gardens.

The first full day of tree transplanting was exhausting.

Coda and I worked past dark, with only the moon and the light of the house guiding us as we lowered the last of the trees into their newly enriched soil. That night, during our labor, I tasted the most savory and most deserved beer and pizza dinner I can remember. We finished and began again the next morning at an early hour, and by the end of the weekend had planted the entire perimeter of the property with twenty trees and perennials. It looked like a "This Old House" transformation. My new neighbors and friends were amazed at what had gone on and when pressed, I admitted to the find. Within a week I was back at the old abandoned nursery, this time to help supply our neighbors' yards with trees as well.

I recently walked through my old home's garden and yard with its current owners, both of whom had watched me plant the entire yard from an adjoining yard and wished for the beauty of the trees and gardens themselves. They had purchased the home from the people that we had sold the house to, after the gardens and yard had been neglected almost to the point of loss. They worked the yard, through love and care, back into additional beauty and now enjoy the shade of trees that stretch for thirty feet into the air and stand out on the prairie for all to see and enjoy. As I walked the yard, I felt blessed that a careful gardener had been at work in my first real labor of love in the soil. The owners offered to allow me to recapture some of the beautiful iris and other very special plantings from my father's and NayNay's gardens that were now gracing their yard. To place such plantings in my current yard, which as yet did not have any of my favorites, meant so much. Some of the original perennials that NayNay had given me will soon become gifts back to her. She has since moved from the beautifully stretching gardens of her home of many years, and with the proper plan and nourishing care I will one day be able to split them out and place them in the "low maintenance" terraced gardens of Nay-Nay's new home and help her tend them. To labor in her yard is a privilege and an honor for me. She is the woman who taught me to take my gardening desire and mold it into art. To take my parents' love for the earthy tastes and smells, and create a canvas of art in soil, making it my own. To imprint yet another part of God's garden, and gift my children with the circle of legacy.

Through three house moves I have carried around a chestnut seedling sprout, never larger than two feet tall. For some reason, my mother-in-law has insisted on my digging it up and moving it with my family. I never gained much affection for the little tree, since I had never gotten it to grow well. The last move, weary of asking me if I would remember to dig it out and bring it with us, she asked if I would simply dig it up and return it to her to nurture and to love.

I pondered the chestnuts that I had carried in my pocket from Paris, wondering how long it would take to grow anything of substance from them. I decided that I would purchase a well-established chestnut tree and place it in my back yard instead. In a few years it will provide shade and nuts and memories of Paris. But this decision didn't stop me from pushing the Paris chestnuts down into the soil with the hope that they, too, would grow into trees like those that line the streets of Paris.

TO MY MOTHER

We welcome back the sunny spring,
'Cause we love to hear the birds sing;
The birds they come because they know,
The ground is bare and warm winds blow.
Mother Nature, with outstretched hands
At her portals beckoning stands;
They come, most joyous at the sight,
And dance around in her delight.

How sad, 'twoud be these birds to see
Come back home to the naked tree;
How dulled their song upon the ear
When the loud north wind it could hear,
When the flowers with covers,
Were sleeping in their winter beds
And Mother Nature herself goie,
And no sun smiling at the dawn.

Like a bird in this sorry plight,
Fighting its way with all its might,
On coming home it seems to me,
My dear mother's face not to see;
The rooms are empty and bare,
The furniture has learnt to stare;
Is it all here? Yes, all's in place,
One thing's lacking, "My Mother's Face."

—Lionel A. Matott

VIGNETTE XIII

Datura metel

BOTANICAL NAME

Angel's Trumpet

COMMON NAME

Angel's trumpet is a tender, delicate annual. It grows best in mounds and spreads to three feet in height. It prefers any well-drained sandy soil or earthy loam, and does well in full sun. Space plants at least two feet apart and wait until all danger of frost has passed. The dark green, veined leaves give way and provide a beautiful backdrop to vibrant white trumpet-shaped flowers that bloom all summer. With its glorious white trumpets facing heavenward, angel's trumpet is suitable in growing containers but is especially beautiful as a border and mixed-bed addition. All parts of the plant are poisonous.

When I was a child, I assumed all things in the heavens were organized for God by the angels. That the angels were in charge of those things that seem to defy explanation; that thunder is the result of a perfect strike in a celestial bowling game; that rain is the tears of angels for the sorrows of the earth; that a rainbow created from sun shining through glass means that an angel is whispering in your ear; that the ring of a bell signifies an angel has received wings; and that the trumpet held in the hands of an angel heralds one in transition from earth to Heaven.

When I'm awakened by a morning chorus of birds outside my window, usually I feel a restful peace and fall back into slumber for another five minutes. This morning was slightly different. The birds' symphony began as usual, but soon was overcome by the constant song of a single mourning dove. She sang from my rooftop and seemed to be communicating something. After about fifteen minutes of listening to her song, I felt compelled to lift my tired frame from the downy bed in which my wife still lay.

I crept to the window and looked out. At dinner the night before, my seven-year-old son had posed a poignant question: "Dad, what if one of the birds that sings at my window in the morning sings out of tune? Do the other birds get mad at him?" My wife and I had flashed each other amused smiles. "Some of the birds I hear don't have very good voices," he continued. His innocence had so amused me, and yet why had I never wondered if some birds carried a tune more eloquently than others?

I returned my gaze to the yard below my window. The dark spears of the leaves of angel's trumpets sprouting through the soil soon would be adorned with beautiful white trumpets heralding in summer. Glancing to the vegetable garden, I found myself intent on the small apple tree below. It would produce beautiful golden apples in the months to come, but now was haloed with beautiful pinkish-white flowers.

Suddenly a familiar whisper seemed to come from the yard below—not the kind of secret-filled whisper that we might share with another, but one that was more like an internal communication, yet strangely audible. It seemed to originate in my vegetable garden, near the bench. Hastily I pulled some clothing and a pair of sandals on. As I entered the yard, which was encased in fog, my heart pounded with memory and anticipation. The memory of the first garden visits that I shared with my mother years after she had departed from this earth flooded through me. If only I could catch her on film, it would provide evidence and some comfort to the unbeliever.

I felt the dew on my bare toes. The apple blossoms, mixed with "God's tears," as my children called the rain when they were little, created a scent across the yard. My son stood at his window above me and watched me walking in the dim light across the lawn. I waved, and he looked at me curiously. I must be a constant source of amusement for my children.

I reminisced on my mother's earlier communications to my heart and soul that had changed so much of my outlook on life. One specific outcome of her visits concerned my father, and my immediate need to get involved in his life.

She impressed upon me in this visit that I needed to see to it that her beloved husband, my father, would take the same relish in his life now. He had viewed his life as empty since she left. . . . My father was now realizing that *he had, for years, lived a great deal of his life through her energy, and now that she was gone, he must generate his own. This had been difficult for him to deal with because he had come to rely on her. He was dealing with all of the feelings of grief and anger that he had, for so long, taken a back seat to her when they might have driven together alongside each other. . . . She seemed to be letting me know that it was her desire that I work with my father and help him come into his own. His future was once again an empty book waiting for the author to bring life to its pages, and return to the journey and adventures which could be written in them. I made a commitment to her that I would spend time with him and help him to come forth.* *

When my mother died, it had taken a big emotional toll on all of us. Many of us view death as a poison of sorts. While it is often a release and a welcome transition for the soul of the one leaving the earthly dimension, it is hard for those left behind. I was weary and totally exhausted by the responsibility of decisions and loss. I was forced into a new role within my immediate family: unofficially designated the family caretaker, I was forced to make the tough decisions, with the later consensus of the rest of the family. I eventually retreated, choosing to sluff off the responsibility and hoping that someone else would step up to the challenge. Yet in the early communications in my garden my mother was pushing me toward my father, indicating that I needed to pull in close, to observe an area where I was needed.

*From Justin Matott, *My Garden Visits* (New York: Ballantine Books, 1996), pp. 27–28.

Shortly after my mother's first visits in my garden, an impending storm started to become apparent. I was alarmed to receive a phone call from my older brother: my father had experienced a devastating episode the previous day. From all appearances, my father had undergone some type of stroke or some other debilitating malady. He was in the hospital, and they needed me to come to help determine what to do. When I arrived, my father was strapped to a bed in a psychiatric ward. He had been heavily sedated, and I scarcely recognized the man who lay there in front of me. We were told that he might never recover and would need to live in assisted care from then on.

My father's depression and sorrow over losing his closest friend and wife were more than he had been able to bear. Often death comes without warning, and the regrets that are left are the disappointments, sorrow, and feelings of remorse that those of us still living here on earth feel. Death leaves us without the complete reconciliation that we would wish for had we known of its arrival. For my father, anger, loneliness, and grief had taken a tremendous toll. He had desperately sought solace without the grace of belief in a higher source; eventually he had retreated to a mind-numbing, attempted escape through drink. For several years my father had been living in a silent hell, trapped by the course of a disease that he could not control. I wish that I had been more aware of the severity of his loss and had been there to aid him earlier.

Thank God for the messages from my mother, drawing me back to the man who has become a close friend. When I first saw him in the hospital, he seemed so different that I thought he was someone else: this could not be my father, the man who had raised me, the dad I love.

We took my father to a place where he could focus on his healing. Although it was not a cure for the disease over which he had no control at the time, it did afford a time together for my relationship with my father to come forward as a new plant in the spring born out of the adversity of a previous, much harsher season. When I arrived at the beautiful setting in the mountains, I did so with the intention of seeking the help my father needed. I stayed in the cabin the treatment center provided to be near him. For the next week, my father and I took walks, talked, shared meals together, and became acquainted as friends in a way that we never had before. Just when I had thought I was going to lose him, a new life of friendship was born.

Now my father is hopeful, and his life has been returned to him with a flourish. He is a valuable grandfather to five and a trusted friend and father. We talk on the phone frequently about writing, gardens, and more, and frequently we will remember some of the zany ways of my mother and laugh. We both miss her and now, as I see the blooms of our friendship, I understand so much more the purpose for my mother's early garden visits. I have come to know the man that she had known. It is wonderful to learn who your father is through the eyes of an adult.

The magic of the morning in my garden held me there; I had no desire to leave its boundaries. The crickets cheeped and the stars began to recede from view as the pink glow grew in the eastern sky. Flowers yawned and opened slowly as the earth warmed. Pink fingers stretched across the eastern sky, making the mountains dance in colors of gray, pink, and green and casting a milky haze across the front range of the Rocky Mountains. The sun popped up over the earth and illuminated the rest of the land to the west; the early morning sky had slowly evolved from black to gray to oranges, pinks, and reds and then, for only a brief moment or two, settled into a band the color of wheat, like dust swirling about, until the white of the clouds overtook the sky. Several robins jumped about the lawn looking for worms or other small bugs.

The fog dissipated with the heating rays of the sun and the single mourning dove had ceased to sing, but a familiar presence stayed in the garden with me as I began to weed and to till the soil where plantings were to be spread.

We spend our days on earth with an angel assigned to us. Our guardian angel, so it would seem, trumpets our coming into the hereafter as a celebration of the life that we enjoyed on earth. The angel's trumpet is a sign that we all will have a time when our bodies will return to the earth and our spirits will soar above it to join in the Master's plan. On the wings of angels we are lifted from our heavy earth "suits" and our Creator brings us "home" with great anticipation.

I believe that the sound of an angel's trumpet can be heard by those who leave this globe when it is their time to enter the incredible reward for displaying faithfulness to God's plan in their lives. To enter a garden beyond our ability to describe.

Brunfelsia calycina floribunda

BOTANICAL NAME

Yesterday, Today, Tomorrow

COMMON NAME

This plant is native to Brazil and is the first shrub that will be introduced to my greenhouse upon its completion. The plant requires humid conditions and acidic soil, and prefers dappled sunlight or shady conditions. It requires great care and pruning to hold its shape, and will grow to a height of ten feet if desired. The leaves grow to four inches with a variety of color—predominantly dark green above with pale green beneath. It takes its lovely name from the fact that its blossoms change color quickly from purple (yesterday), to lavender (today), and finally to white (tomorrow). The flowers, which gather in masses of tubular shapes, are borne in great clusters and bloom abundantly in the spring. In a nontropical setting the evergreen shrub will lose most of its foliage for a short period of time.

This is the only plant in this book that I have not yet grown myself. It is the symbol of the future for me, and for the work of my tending during the colder months of the year. I am dedicated to building a greenhouse and starting new memories within it. The yesterday, today, tomorrow will hold a place of prominence in the greenhouse, a dedication to all those I love, a symbol of their ongoing relevance in my life. When I look upon the plant in the artificially created tropical environment, I will remember the days that have led to this point, focus on the things that I can affect now, and look forward to the lessons still to be learned and the times to come.

AH, SPRING IS COME, with promises of renewal, the chance to begin fresh again with a new palette, and the opportunity to turn and till the soil for a new future harvest. This is the time for the resurrection of both soul and soil, the time to allow for the hopes, imagination, and possibilities of a new season. The first day of spring is like New Year's Day with its strange, magic yarns that allow us to ponder the ways that we can improve on our past performances. Yards are full of corms, tubers, bulbs, and rhizomes bursting from the soil with new life and vigor. Commonly known to us as tulips, daffodils, hyacinths, crocuses, bluebells, lilies, irises, colchicum, aconite, snowdrops, allium, anenome, begonias, canna, dahlias, cyclamen, freesia, gladiolus, and gloxinias, their flowers are welcome friends after a long winter.

All of our yesterdays make up all of our todays, which will, tomorrow, become our yesterdays. The past, present, and future are inseparable, their well-worn patterns drawn out in the fabric of relationships. Life is a circle of events and impressions left indelibly by the humans that carry God's messages. I look at the landscape of legacy etched across the faces of my children and realize that their mannerisms and the way they hold themselves are a culmination of their experiences mingled with my wife's and mine. I determine to make their tomorrows brighter by focusing on their todays.

One of my sons asked if he could clip some of the new tulips for his teacher; my other son talked of a vegetable stand this summer. He wanted to set up a small shop where he could earn some extra money, and promised to help plant the garden this year and even pay for some seeds so that he could claim all the profits.

I remembered my own youthful eagerness to share the fruits of the garden—and to earn extra spending money. In the spring and summer of my childhood, my father would allow me to cut flowers from his gardens, which I would push around in my small red wagon door to door, selling fresh-cut flowers at some ridiculously low price. In the summer my cart would overflow with fresh vegetables, and in the fall gourds, pumpkins, and dried flowers would find their way into the homes of our neighbors.

My first stop was to offer payment in kind for the gooseberries and lemonade that a dear elderly friend had always bestowed on me so graciously. The vegetables were always a reminder to her of a time gone by, when her back still allowed her to plant and tend at the earth's level. Another dear elderly woman lived farther down the lane from our house. She was a sweet and kindly woman as well. With all her children and grandchildren living in another state, she welcomed me into her home. Her house always smelled of oil paint and baking, the oil paint odor emanating from her many canvases that lay all around her spacious living room in some state of drying or awaiting more of her hand. She would often tell me that I had a beautiful face and feed me warm chocolate chip cookies or hot chocolate. I would give her a complimentary bouquet that I would handcraft myself from my father's garden; it was usually graced with the sunflowers and wheat cuttings that stretched out for miles around the countryside near my home. She painted several of the bouquets that I had given her. Unbeknownst to me at the time, she also was painting me as I sat in her kitchen eating warm cookies and petting her huge cats.

At the end of my last preteen summer, she presented me with the beautiful oil painting. It was like looking into a mirror that only caught my good side—the one that the sweet, lonely old widow saw as she would soak up our visits.

At some point in my later years I sold the painting with a lot of other childhood treasures that I had collected on my journeys, including a collection of several hundred 45-rpm records that I wish I had now—classics like "The Lion Sleeps Tonight," "Heartaches by the Numbers," and "Your Cheating Heart," which I would listen to over and over on an old turntable in the privacy of my room. I would love to have the sweet painting back now, along with all my other treasures that I traded, no doubt for something much less valuable.

The earth in spring sings of its creative powers and energy. It suits itself in a banquet of color as if preparing a celebration for God and humanity. The amazing awakening is something that gardeners everywhere look forward to with great anticipation each winter when the cold winds blow, and rain and snow cover the land, and the trees stretch toward heaven in their naked dance. The winter holds many beauties in its own right, but the cold is something that the body can never become fully accustomed to; this is the reason we look forward to the warmer months to come. The spring comes slowly and gently melts back the waters frozen by the cold months and awakens our senses to life's priority and balance.

This morning, the earth came alive to me. A full moon the previous night must have contributed to the overall serenity. I ran along the valley west of my house, in new running shoes, with a resolve to participate actively in personal growth and have a more loving attitude toward the human race. As I jogged along the pathway, I encountered spring. The crabapple trees burst forth in blossom, and the grasses reached heavenward. A cool morning rain released the scents from the warming earth, and when mixed with the dogwood, crabapple, and wild flower blossoms that beautified the running path, took me back once again to a simpler time in my life. A time when the pressures of jobs, family commitments, and bills were not keeping my eyes constantly focused on the forward events, instead of relishing the moment I was in. A time when the here-and-now was as important as any future considerations and therefore allowed me to grasp the enormous possibility of God's creation and the beauty set aside for those of His people who allow rest to invade their otherwise too busy routines.

There is so much wrong with the world now and so much reported daily that invades our sense of well-being that we forget that we truly, in many ways, still inhabit the garden of Eden that God intended for us from the start. When we slow down enough to meditate on those things that are right with the world, we understand how much of heaven, of Eden, is still among us. And every day not accounted for is a loss.

Life can be brutal—it holds no guarantees other than that we will experience change—but we must learn to relish the life we have here because, in a time not so distant, we too will depart this dimension, possibly still longing to taste the smells, sights, and experiences of earth. I do believe that the other side is preferable to this one because I think it will be devoid of all the sorrows and bitterness we encounter here. Nevertheless, as much as we can, we must relish the time here and spend it wisely. Yesterdays cannot be altered; todays and tomorrows can.

As I ran along this new morning, the sun peeked over the eastern landscape, bringing a pink glow to the mountains, like being in an overturned bowl of strawberry milk. I reached toward the mountains, coming closer to them with each step. The sky continued to lighten, adding new colors to the landscape. Warm pockets of air mingled with the remnants of cooler air hanging still from the previous night. As the world lightened, I saw I shared the path with small "roly poly" bugs searching out food or refuge; small caterpillars were reaching toward the opposite side. I chuckled to myself, wondering if the grass looked greener to the caterpillars on the other side of the path. To one side, a small cottontail rabbit, no larger than my fist, jumped onto the path and scurried ahead of me. Years ago, my childhood dog would leap out and sprint in vain to catch the hundreds of cottontail rabbits that lived in the vast fields about my home.

I jogged along a creek bank lined with huge cottonwood

trees, and the air came alive with the songs of the meadowlarks and robins. The meadowlark, with its beautiful, dandelion-colored breast, creates one of the loveliest songs in nature. I slowed to a walk and then sat under one of the trees and watched a pair of meadowlarks as they communicated over the span of one hundred yards. He, in a pine tree, would call to her in a melodious, almost mournful song. She, in turn, would call to him in a slightly more cheerful song from across the stream in an old cottonwood tree. They "spoke" to each other for the twenty minutes I observed them. I remembered a time many years ago, when I lay in the top bunk of the beds that my brother and I shared for years. It was an early summer morning, and I could hear my father across the gravel road priming the pump near the pond that supplied the surrounding yards and gardens with the sustenance that would ensure survival in the hot summer days to follow. The meadowlarks were singing joy-fully in the tree holding my tree house, and somewhere deep in my heart and soul I associated the meadowlark song with se-renity and peace and a good place in the world. Now when I hear the sound of the meadowlark I involuntarily say a quick and thankful prayer for life's simple pleasures.

Every winter I long for the first day that the meadow-larks' songs will come to me on an early morning jog. The day that I hear them for the first time in the season I know that the world is well and that spring has come again. It doesn't matter what circumstances surround me, good or bad—that day is always a lighter and more celebrated day for me. Yester-day, today, and tomorrow—all have come.

TO THE VIOLET

Lovely little Maiden, with thy face so blue,
Kissed by golden sunbeams, sprinkled by the dew,
Loved by the morning, blessed by evening star,
Guarded by the pale moon, shining from afar,
Pleased to smile from spots where no footsteps fall,
In meadow or on sunny banks where the grass grows tall;
Shyest of all flowers, loveliest, most fair,
Lending thy faint perfume to the bonny air,
Teach me, little maiden, thy own purity,
So I might live like thee in security.

—Lionel A. Matott

*Each morning I awaken to the face of
an older man and I pray for his wisdom
for the coming day.*

Like life, few gardens have only flowers.
—Anonymous

THE LAST OF A heavy, wet spring snow has just one last remnant left in my yard, a small strip of soil that the sun doesn't reach because of the branches of a thick evergreen. The front garden is alive, bees buzzing as they travel between grape hyacinth, daffodils, tulips, pansies, crocuses, and early irises, collecting elixir. The bulbs that I pressed below the loam have once again pushed up and have met the new season with tender, eager blooms. The earth is alive with beauty; the winter has retreated. My dog, Snickers, sits, relishing the warming sun on her coat and panting. I click away on my laptop computer unaware of the tennis balls that Snickers has set at my feet. Her nose twitches constantly as new fragrances pour from the earth. The nectar from the hyacinth, a sweet grapey scent, wafts in the air as the sun warms the flowers, and all of the surrounding earth. The rest of the yard is silent, save for the birds, an occasional plane, and the soft buzzing of the bees. Energy and life had returned to the earth, and yet I realized it had never left. Among the slighter sounds of many small bees buzzing about the flower garden comes the low rumbling of a large honeybee. I watch in fascination as he glides between the upturned faces of pansies, tulips, and the last of the grape hyacinths; he then finds my columbines nestled in between tall iris shoots. He performs a dance, each of the flower heads bowed as he rests on their petals and, as if kissing each flower, collects for later.

Every so often when I truly allow the quiet to invade my life, to pierce through the otherwise noisy activity that so often consumes us, I get small glimpses of the original garden where we were intended to live. Toiling with the earth and turning over our soil and souls is hard, often painful, work, but our labors often bear fruit; Eden is near.

I sat on the bench and meditated for some time. I thought of how my mother and father had taught me to respect others, particularly women. I thought of the gift of intuition that women have and the respect for all things that seems more innate to them than to us men with our seemingly mostly rough-and-tumble thoughts. I thought of the fortunate state that men in our society have now over our ancestors, since it is now more accepted that men be tender and loving to their children and wives, not simply providers, cavemen. Men have come a long way, and yet we still have a long way to go to match the plan that our Creator mapped out for us. His original plan was for us to be gardeners. Gardeners tend to be gentle sorts with a deep understanding of the earth from which they have sprung. That is why I think so many of us love the time in the garden and why many are again awakening to its promise and cathartic capabilities in an often harsh world.

The early morning's sights and sounds in a garden are enchanting. Spending time in the garden by only a receding moon, starlight, and the beginning of a sunrise allows for a totally different perspective on life. The gray, black, and white tones allow the imagination to take over, to create its own colors. I enjoy getting up in the spring and summer months before daybreak, to tend my garden in the earliest dawn and then to jog along vegetated paths while the air is still cool and the sun is awakening to the east.

I look at the surrounding weeds when I run along my familiar path. Weeds that were small become knee high, and will continue up until their genetic code tells them to cease. One particular weed that infiltrates the grassy banks in a nearby canyon produces thousands of small yellow flowers about three feet off the ground; from a distance it looks like a tremendous meadow of lemons, and every so often a tuft of red Indian paintbrush peeks up, showing me a masterful design at work. The fields are nothing more and nothing less than a spreading garden, the caretaker watchful.

Our time on this earth is precious. If we all will focus on the positive even when the storms on our horizon look impossible, we can overcome and live fuller and richer lives. In my life I have chosen to reflect on the positive aspects of people and my relationships with them. As with any relationship, there are many bumps and bruises along the way; it is the interaction that is important, the love and the forgiveness so that we can live fully and happily. To keep short accounts of the wrongs and long memories of the right things about people, with the hope that we, too, will be forgiven our own inadequacies. For a life is truly like a garden: each holds import and the ability to leave an imprint like no other. The cultivation of lovely and often fleeting events builds for a future that will, in some small way, change the world back closer to the design of Eden.

La-da-deee, la-da-da. . . .

Not the End, for Love Is Eternal . . .

ABOUT THE AUTHOR

JUSTIN MATOTT lives, writes, gardens, and raises his family in Colorado. *A Harvest of Reflections* is his second book. He is also the author of a children's book, *Ol' Lady Grizelda*.

For comments or information about the work of Mr. Matott, please contact:

P.O. Box 261183
Littleton, Colorado 80163-1183